To my lovely mum Tilly.

One of the last of a sparkling generation.

Biography

Wallace Fields was born in Liverpool; studied piano under Claire Pollard, and later under Bert Hayes where he studied jazz harmony; and at the age of fourteen quickly established himself on the thriving Liverpool cabaret circuit as an accompanist. Whilst a student at the London School of Economics he played in the student "Trad" Band, made some appearances with the famed Cy Laurie band in Soho, and wrote music for a film about the LSE.

He spent some years teaching and lecturing in Political History; and for many years played "Cocktail" piano on the posh West End Hotel Circuit including residencies at the "Intercontinental" "Meridian" "Inn on the Park" "Berners Hotel" and "Braganza".

In 1980 he formed the Jewish Music Group (JMG) which played a mixture of Yiddish Jazz, and his own compositions set to the Hebrew Poetry of Rachel Blaustein and Shaul Tchernikovski. He also wrote poetry, for translation into Hebrew and performed with his own especially written compositions. One such number "Har Zion Yerushalayim" (Mount Zion) was performed by his group "Klezmer Swingers" at "Ronnie Scott's" as a tribute to Ronnie Scott the day after his death.

His interest in Jewish Culture led to his setting up the "Redbridge Festival of Jewish Music" and the "Ram Theatre Company" in 1981 which together initiated the now thriving UK Jewish Cultural Renaissance. In 1994 He formed the "Klezmer Swingers" which (together with "Klezmer Groove") led the UK Klezmer revival. The Klezmer Swingers have performed at major Concert Halls, Theatres, and Festivals throughout the UK including "Ronnie Scott's" and "100 Club" London West End. Moving easily between the worlds of Jewish Culture, Klezmer and Jazz, he has also written a number of Operettas on Jewish themes including the popular "Klnneret" which has been performed both at the Mayfair Theatre London. and at the London South Bank Centre. It also undertook a highly successful tour of Israel in 1986. In 2003 he formed the "Wally Fields Jazz Orchestra" and was received with the distinction of a sold-out performance at the prestigious South Bank with many "promenaders" paying to stand in the Aisles! Subsequent appearance there have regularly sold out including a special Concert sponsored by the Polish Cultural Institute (Polish Foreign Ministry) which featured Fields' "Partizan Rhapsody" in tribute to the fighters of the Warsaw Ghetto uprising of 1943. Fields' "Concerto in Jazz" followed and is now also regularly performed. The WFJO opened the 2007 season at the Liverpool Philharmonic Hall for their celebration of the 800th anniversary of the founding of Liverpool, and also to celebrate the Liverpool Capital of Culture Year 2008.

When not performing, or composing, Fields enjoys nothing better than Art Galleries, Film Noir, and the Café society of Hampstead. Currently (2013) he is working on the Libretto and musical score for his "Burlesque Operetta" Theodor set in "fin de Siecle" Vienna of 1900.

Wally Fields Jazz Orchestra

Wallace Fields, Jenny Howe, James Pearson.

Klezmer Swingers

Ronnie Scott's 1997
Ronnie, Wally, Malcolm, Murray, Paul.

Wallace Fields

FASTOVSKI'S TALES OF HAMPSTEAD
and
Significant Reminiscences of Misspent Youth

AUSTIN MACAULEY PUBLISHERS™

LONDON · CAMBRIDGE · NEW YORK · SHARJAH

A CIP catalogue record for this title is available from the British Library.

ISBN 9781398497559 (Paperback)
ISBN 9781398497566 (Hardback)
ISBN 9781398497580 (ePub e-book)
ISBN 9781398497573 (Audiobook)

www.austinmacauley.com

First Published 2023
Austin Macauley Publishers Ltd®
1 Canada Square
Canary Wharf
London
E14 5AA

Table of Contents

Fastovski's chance encounter with the proprietor of a Polish Delicatessen takes him back in time to the Jewish Bakeries of wartime Liverpool, and how he eats a giant juice-oozing sour cucumber wrapped in brown paper whilst walking up Brownlow Hill...and sings with the famous Jewish comedian Issy Bonn at the Pavilion Theatre. The notorious incident is related of the bacon sandwich, Paul of Tarsus, and "Big Dave" Rusnak the hooligan Chassid and competent flautist.

The eccentric and crazed multi-married Lancastrian Uncle who claimed that his feet were back to front, and his even worse cousin Morton the self-declared genius and "Picasso of Southport" who put a sewing machine in every painting. The famed and fearless 86-year-old "Auntie Schwartzwald" faces arrest (yet again) for disturbing the peace...some of the family.

"Issy the Greek" the barber-showman ("Is" is a whizz with the scizz") father to Fastovski, and tales of his Runyanesque cronies "Docker", "The Rajah", "Big Mick" and "Louis the Chink" in downtown wartime Liverpool. The silly "Film Star" Ronald Shiner makes an unfortunate reference to "Jewish conks" at a Jewish ex-servicemen's stag night. His escape is described.

Scots Wha Hey!…Page 70

Fastovski is driven mad by a tin whistle-playing Somali who thinks he is a Scotsman. He remembers leaving a young Paul McCartney covered in bruises from a game of football in the park and describes the antics of the Israeli goalkeeper who was sent off for clinging to the crossbar and much to the annoyance of his mother.

Whatever happened to Terry Tan?…Page 80

Fastovski reminisces about his Liverpool schooldays and his uber-sadistic Gestapo-trained Hebrew teachers; bloodshed in the playground and fights with the local schools. Jews loudly slurping Chinese Food at "Kwok Fongs" eating house; from whence a young Terry Tan is sent to the Hebrew School (aka "The Slaughterhouse") to become an Englishman…with some predictable results.

Moss Bros…Page 99

The most violent and comic game of football in the history of the world, leaving the Ref literally buried alive beneath the pitch after attempting to intercede between the fiery Moss Brothers. The Lord Mayor of Liverpool knocks out the Centre forward and Hindenburg strangles the centre half. Fastovski fondly recalls his acapella singing group being ordered from a concert hall for the crime of singing "Davy Crockett" out of tune and recounts the strange story of Reverend Wolfe when he met Ivan the Terrible on the top floor of a Liverpool Bus…

Warrior Avyn...Page 118

Fastovski gives his prams' eye view of the Liverpool Blitz of May 1941 and the stylish jazz café society of the time, and compares it with the new more lumpen Liverpool of 2006; where an encounter is related with an aggressive waitress bearing an uncanny resemblance to Mr Wayne Rooney the footballer. Bring back the war!

Popper's Private Army...Page 138

Fastovski and his dissipated cohorts Palevski, Codrington-Ball and "Wild Jim" career from the "Three Tuns Bar" at the London School of Economics to a yeshivah at Stamford Hill via a Ferrari showroom in Baker Street, Popski's Private Army, Professor Karl Popper (and Mrs Popper...who Fastovski would visit in the afternoons) the Manchurian Crisis of 1931, Dylan Thomas, Kafka, Machiavelli and death at the dartboard... Jazz, sex, "Fremlins" ale and Taffy the Barman from Connemara.

Ward...Page 160

Fastovski is rushed to hospital where he meets a Welsh Chinese fantasist and a teddy-boy-Iranian-Episcopalian-trainee-priest whose father had lost his false teeth at Heathrow. An old mad German locum consultant terrorises the ward and Fastovski remembers rolling drunk from a synagogue reception at the age of fourteen with his pal "Cake" Wassermann whose father had been awarded the iron cross for speaking Yiddish... Fastovski is visited by Long John Silver, Robert Newton and the Duke of Edinburgh and trades in both a wife and girlfriend for the pretty blonde nurse.

The Red Shadow...Page 174

Fastovski sings with Anne Ziegler and Webster Booth at a Barricade under attack in Paris, and escapes to join the French Foreign Legion whilst disguised as Pantomime Cat. Joining the Cast of "Desert Song" by Sigmund Romberg, he fights off the advances of the Rif Tribesmen (having previously fought off advances of a different nature in Bradford).

Confederate Liverpool...Page 185

Fastovski's reminiscences of a vibrant bustling Liverpool in the 1860s and its symbiotic relationship with the Confederate South in the American Civil War.

Synopsis

Fastovski reminisces with deep irony on his misspent youth in a long-gone Jewish Liverpool, whilst sipping assam tea in the cafés of leafy Hampstead. Surrounded by characters from the merely manic to the mainly maniac, he recounts his recollections of these exotic and singular people, and the absurd situations in which they act out their lives around him.

His father the barber/showman "Issy the Greek" and his wildly eccentric family are described in much loving detail, including the crazed Lancastrian Uncle Hymie (who claimed that his feet were back to front), his grandfather Elimelech (unrestrained Lothario and fanatical supporter of Southport FC), and brother-in-law Shrolik (who disapproved somewhat of his activities)…both "tough guys" and veterans of the Russo-Japanese War and volunteers in the British Army in 1914.

The precocious infant Fastovski gives his pram's eye view of the Liverpool Blitz of May 1941 with all the assurance of an Ed Morrow or an Alistair Cooke and recalls the jazz musician family of his mother Tilly and his grandmother Lena with the piercing green eyes who loved Jesus.

His own career as young rapscallion is recalled, with his penchant for persecuting the Liverpool Jewish Rabbinate, and his strong friendship with the iconoclastic Reverend "Willy" Wolfson, Mountain Jew and human being, from Tredegar in South Wales. His career as second team captain for Liverpool Haroldeans Football Club with violent and hilarious consequences is glowingly recalled; as are his adventures as a student at the London School of Economics together with his somewhat dissipated cohorts Palevski, Codrington-Ball and "Wild Jim".

Chapter One
Bartek's Apple Pie

Fastovski could not sleep. He had retired to bed at the usual time (anywhere between 8pm to 8am, to be precise) and really had tried his best to nod off. However, he simply could not make that transition from the domain of terror and guilt which he inhabited, and into the comforting sanctuary of straightforward good and honest nightmare which somehow kept itself at minds length. Not that he had tried to induce that state of other-consciousness by artificial means such as barbiturates, a large slug of Remy or even the old stand-bye of imagined Antipodeans pursuing sheep (and rams even) over hurdles, ditches and mountain edges...and such like (which did sometimes work). No, he simply closed his eyes, induced a yawn and settled down to a hopefully awaited troubled unconscious... If not the "chief nourisher in life's feast" as Macbeth would have it, then certainly the pickled herring before the salt beef; the barley soup before the boiled flank; or the pigs cheek before the chitterlings and hominy grits of life itself. He ruminated for a while as to whether this latter dish could be ordered at the Savoy Grill, without inviting a devastating raised eyebrow from Carlo, the head waiter, and comforted himself with the notion that most certainly the then American ambassador, Averell Harriman no doubt fortified himself with that splendid dish prior to his well-known tryst with that other splendid dish (and daughter in-law of Winston Churchill) at the Savoy Grill in the grimly beautiful days of 1941 or thereabouts... What then did the young lady order? Perhaps a light lettuce salad, some boiled chicken (with a little mange tout) and maybe a half bottle of Krug...at least this is what Fastovski was now musing as he turned over, then under; inwards and outwards for the umpteenth time, and all in a vain attempt to escape his train of thought.

The problem...was Bartek. Not **strictly** Bartek, but his apple pie... You see, some days previously Fastovski had happened upon a little Polish delicatessen near to the Heath, but otherwise in a road of some innocuity.

Anyway, the sight and aroma of this "food of heroes" was simply too much for the poor chap who staggered into the portals of Bartek's emporium with all the zeal and indeed fanaticism of a fourteenth century French flagellant through the doors of Rouen Cathedral, seeking some relic of the host. I swear. 'Whatya got,' he shouted, trembling and shaking with emotion. Bartek (who was no fool) immediately understood what was called for and, looking directly into Fastovski's black and penetrating eyes (a little red with emotion by this time, and somewhat rolling around his head in the throes of food frenzy); addressed him in a steady, calm and reassuring voice which had been tried and tested on various sections of Polish manhood in similar circumstances back in Gdansk. '*Ve heve Cracov sawsaj...a vondairful serlection of hems, boyeld and smokd...ve arlso heve sawps ...barley sawp, pea sawp...hherrrrrings...and of course... kike...seemply vondairfool kike!*'

'What sort of cake?' said Fastovski, almost anticipating the answer but dreading the possibility of his expectations being dashed by any momentary non-availability.

'Vell, my frend,' said Bartek; now sensing that he was in control of this potentially dangerous situation. 'Vell, Vee heve poppysid kike…and…eppel pie. Apple pie! Apple PIE!' screamed Fastovski. 'Yers…eppel pie,' responded Bartek with a cat-like smile, and the merest suggestion of a sigh of relief. He could now remove his foot from the panic button that connected him to the Hampstead Police Station, just up the hill.

Fastovski at this juncture began to feel some abatement in his food panic. Bartek meanwhile (and in increasing confidence) began to regale him with details of the regional varieties of Boar sausage in the fastnesses of the Carpathian Mountains and also Fulham (from whence apparently Bartek shipped in his supplies of apple and other pies from an emigre Polish baker (and boar sausage processor) every Saturday, and the delights of cream cheese from Bialystock, to Bermondsey no doubt. Fastovski missed all of this simply because he had ceased to listen…just as well really. God knows what crazed romantic notions he was entertaining in his food-fevered brain about the Polishness of the said apple pie; which however, the merest association with Fulham of all places…would irrevocably destroy…forever! Whilst Bartek continued "in accelerando" in his reverie on the genius of Polish food, Fastovski fixed him with a look of solemn and totally insincere attentiveness and with a mind completely dead to the increasing ravings of a now manically energised Bartek; who, had he not lost himself by now in the historical antecedents of beetroot and horseradish "chrein" (as the Jews would have it), would and indeed should have observed the glazed expression that Fastovski was wearing and his rapid transformation from a state of previous high animation to one now of stone-faced immobility. In short, Fastovski was now completely indistinguishable from the great Golem of Prague. Probably, Bartek had he been aware of this might have altered his strange syntax somewhat, but he wasn't, so he didn't.

Fastovski's mind as could be perceived was elsewhere...in his home town of Liverpool to be exact, and, as a small child visiting one of the great Jewish Bakers which at that time were in full evidence in a thriving Cosmopolitan Port City (bit like Hamburg really with its great German cafés, restaurants and food shops which had all but disappeared after the differences of opinion in 1914...indeed Adolf himself had relatives there whom he visited in 1911) Yes, a pulsating City with a vibrant, irreverent and generally "offbeat" Jewish community. "Silver's Bakery" also had masses of herrings in deep oak barrels with ratchety (and not very clean) old Jewish women digging deep with rolled up sleeves in an effort to find a superior specimen...much to the disgust of the more fastidious customers (including Fastovski's mother) who was treating her offspring to the Jewish culinary delights of Brownlow Hill on the day after his Uncle Joe had taken him to watch Liverpool near the Kop End at Anfield, and where the right back Ray Lambert had booted the ball up field (sometimes accompanied by an opposing player or two) from the sanctuary of the penalty area all through the game, whilst his voluminous and famous shorts would have done credit to Old Mother Riley if not Two Ton Tessie O'Shea (whom he resembled somewhat) and where his craggy wax-like visage, grim set jaw and bald shining bonce set themselves into the psyche of young Fastovski as a role model and ubermensch. In fact, for a time in later years, Fastovski himself played football very much in this vein in the Northern Jewish Soccer League; where any accusation that his rough tactics could be likened to that of Ray Lambert would in fact be treated as a most effusive compliment. Where were we? Oh. Yes, all the things that Bartek was by now increasingly raving about were in the main to be had at "Silvers" although to be frank there was little evidence of sausage made from wild, or any other type of Boar for that matter. No, it would neither be available from Jewish shops nor eaten at home, where the community-maintained kosher.

There was, however, a comfortable and implied understanding between the local Rabbinate and the Community whereby a traditional home-based orthodoxy was observed but where outside of the home…well "anything goes" was the order of the day. This pact of Jesuitical-like hair splitting manifested itself mainly in the (generally surreptitious) devouring of fried bacon, concealed if possible, under the fried egg and tomatoes until the very last second in local restaurants whilst keeping a wary eye out in the event that "you were seen". This humanitarian attitude to pork consumption did not extend to a public and open display, but nevertheless tacitly accepted the furtive, secretive and somewhat hurried meal that Jews in Liverpool would eat. Not for them a nice lingering meal as the Christians enjoyed. The Jews never actually had time to savour the aroma of this powerful, smoky, salty delicatessen. See it and get it down while nobody's looking…that was the order of the day.

Bartek was still rabbiting on…literally. Apparently, he was a fanatic for "Lapin Fume" (Polish style, naturally) and failed to observe that the Golem standing transfixed at the other side of the counter was salivating slightly. Not I hasten to add, dribbling, but *salivating!* You see, Fastovski was now walking out of "Silvers" and proceeding up Brownlow Hill clutching a huge sour cucumber in a brown paper bag whilst quickly endeavouring to swallow the juice, the acid, the "Rossel" as the Jews referred to it; before it ran down his hands and up his sleeves and into the gutter and went wastefully to its dilution with the even more noxious chemicals in the River Mersey. Fastovski regarded the cucumber and proceeded to demolish it with gusto…the great wet pips the size of threepenny bits; the wonderfully thick, green and eruptive skin as near to that of a toad as could be obtained in the entire world of Jewish vegetables.

A gentle stroll followed through the Victorian splendours of Rodney Street (the Harley Street of Liverpool) and into Hardman Street where an open topped number five tram thereupon conducted them past the Philharmonic, up Parliament Street and its newly bombed elegant Georgian Terraces and thence up to sinister Lodge Lane from whence the tram with its smells of oil, and old wood, and mint imperials went cluttering and swaying on its tracks all the way down Smithdown Road, past the cemetery and on to the junction with Ullet Road where the two alighted, into a steady drizzle. Fastovski adored the rain and resisted the urgings of his mother to cover himself up, and let it beat down upon his face and neck, and into his rough woolly socks with the red band around the top which were commonly worn at the time by small boys of his ilk.

Back past "Axelrods" (the grocer), "Tiffenbergs" (the butcher), "Viner" (the fishmonger), "Jumps" (the greengrocer) and "Masons Sweetshop" where the best Sarsaparilla and Dandelion and Burdock in the entire world was to be obtained…not forgetting "Tizer" and "Sticky Lice". Years later, Polly's Milk Bar would open opposite "Masons" (next door to the ladies Hairdresser "Maison Gwladys"), and where Fastovski downed his first Coca Cola and hated it instantly. Polly would provide discreet bacon sandwiches, ("chazzer" in the yiddish, as the Jewish lads would refer to it), well hidden in thick crusty white bread where from even a short distance the contents could not be ascertained, except for the smell of course. Until one day that is when Fastovski and some of his pals were recuperating after a hard nights drinking at the "Jacaranda" and were gorging the therapeutic benefits of "Polly's Chazzer Banjo's" (as one of the boys back from National Service in the jungles of Malaya referred to them), when presumably because of the ribaldry of the boys, and the heady smell of the chazzer, Polly for one brief but cataclysmic moment slightly lowered her guard, and shouted from the kitchen to advise Fastovski that his **BACON** sandwich would be ready in "a tick" or in "half a mo", whatever. Fate decreed that at the moment who should walk in but Big Dave Rusnak, who was not only one of the toughest Jews in Liverpool…a thug really…and who was incidentally a very fine musician and flautist. That was not the problem. Being a thug, Jewish or even a flute player would provide no grounds of incompatibility with the great food of the Goyim. Perhaps, Fastovski mused…perhaps this was what constituted Pauls conversion on the way to Damascus…a whoppin' great chazzer banjo served by some Levantinine fellow in a tarboosh, whilst Paul slyly concealed his prayer shawl, doffed the yarmulke on his head and scoffed the aforementioned forbidden sarnie…Fastovski and numerous fellow Jews had experienced the same blinding white light after their first bite of a bacon sarnie…a light so graphically described by Paul in his deluded religious context. The fact that this most likely version was not mentioned in Pauls Epistle to the Gentiles; did not (at least to Fastovski) mean that the event had not taken place. In fact it was, Fastovski considered, a far more credible explanation for the spawning of the entire ethos of Christianity than the rather weird imaginings of the Immaculate Conception; which however, is still accepted wholeheartedly in wide sections of the Church…but not in Hampstead…thank God.

Anyway, in walks Big Dave Rusnak just (as you will remember) Polly was announcing the imminent birth of Fastovski's sandwich (well buttered incidentally and with a large libation of HP brown sauce added as was his wont.) The problem, and it certainly *was* a problem, was that Big Dave was adorned in the garb of a Chassid. Not only garbed as such but as quickly became evident he actually now *was* a Chassid. Nobody had seen Dave for a while, and rumours had gone round that he had forsaken the world of Scarlatti, Debussy, Mozart and the Magic Flute (and also bashing people up in bar room brawls in the dubious taverns of Lime

Street and Scotland Road of a Friday night)...and had undergone his own version of the Pauline Conversion, but completely in reverse (well, he commenced as a fairly normal, albeit somewhat violent Scouse Yid, and had transmogrified into a rabbinical student at a Yeshivah in Gateshead where he prayed and studied Torah all day long. (No bacon, no boozing, no shikses, no brawls) A total withdrawal of everything (possibly with the exception of the flute) that constituted the various components of Mr David Rusnak. A sort of Big Dave-less Big Dave; if you follow my meaning.

Fastovski had the presence of mind to shout quickly to Polly (whilst ensuring that the instruction was in ear-shot of Dave) that she must have made a mistake, and that the sandwich was destined for somebody else. This created a further problem in that the entire clientele was Jewish and obviously all present in pursuit of the same purpose, and which set up further vigorous denials all round as to the paternity it seemed, of the now abandoned "chazzer banjo" which looked quite forlorn. The ex-soldier had been bragging about one of his experiences with a Malaysian Nurse and had seemed to be the only one oblivious to the entrance of Big Dave. However, on catching sight of the now black hatted, black kaftaned shaven headed bearded and black booted Dave; the poor unfortunate could do no other, it seems than open his mouth in shock. Unfortunately, the ex-soldier had been munching his own bacon sarnie with some great gusto and a rasher stuck out of his mouth and onto his chin like a tongue afflicted with some of the nastier manifestation of the great plagues of Egypt...well more like a rasher of good streaky which indeed itwas.

D'ye know the cartoons of HM Bateman. You do? Well, it was something like that. Dave regarded the soldier and spoke (quite softly) to him whilst feigning to disregard the offending piece of pig sticking out from underneath his not inconsiderable proboscis whilst everybody literally stopped breathing. To add to the horror the ex-soldier was caught on the horns of a dilemma, and considerably worse (he later confided) for him than the debacle occasioned to his British Army forebears on the Horns of Hattin, where Saladin himself expressed his own singular disapproval of the bacon tendency. He too feigned to disregard the offending article which thereupon continued to wag up and down in rhythm with his chin whilst in the course of a seemingly innocuous conversation. It was no less than a tableau of majestic social embarrassment…of heroic magnitude. Dave eventually took his leave after exchanging a few anodyne and light remarks, but remarkably without leaving knuckle marks all round, as indeed had been generally feared. The ex-soldier confessed later that he would have sooner faced the Communist Guerilla's in the Malayan Jungle (and no doubt the nurse) then ever again encounter Big Dave, the only Chassid in Liverpool as bad luck would have it and in such circumstance.

Fastovski and his mother reached the house only minutes after alighting from the tram, with his mother rekindling the fire whilst Fastovski sat in front of it with steam rising from his wet socks, and reading the comic strip adventures of Issy Bonn and the Finkelfeffer family in "The Radio Fun". This was of some resonance for the young man as only weeks before he had sung a little song about raspberry jam with the famed Issy on the stage of the Pavilion Theatre in Liverpool, and for his pains had been awarded the prize of…yes…a pot of Raspberry Jam. "Keillers" it was, and very good too. He had been urged onto the stage despite his protestations, by his father (also called "Issy" by coincidence)…and a well-known showman around the thriving Liverpool club scene at the time. Anyhow, he put the comic down and started to munch on a piece of home-made apple pie which his mother kept for occasions such as these…or indeed any occasions at all when Fastovski (and mouth) were present. In a way his mother had urged on him a form of apple pie dependency which in its intensity exceeded the worst cases of cocaine injecting which at that time was looked upon with horror (See Vincent Price in the film "Dragonwyk" c1944). When Fastovski grew up somewhat, and broadened his experience of confectionary all the way from almond slice to windbeutal, he could never quite forget his first love of apple pie, and when he began to engage in affairs of the heart and, as sometimes could happen, he found his affections to be unreciprocated; he would as likely drown his sorrows in a hundredweight of apple pie as in a flagon of Remy.

Indeed like Bartek, Fastovski was no fool although he very often appeared to act like one, and indeed he did recall that due to his obsessive behaviour concerning this confection from Valhalla, he was prone not to take himself nor life seriously enough. It was in fact only whilst daydreaming through Bartek's monologue that he realised his parents had never provided a suitable alternative… something of permanence for him to turn to in moments of unhappiness; say, like a teddy bear which several of his friends possessed, but nevertheless kept quiet about. Indeed looking back at the young man with the wet socks, he recognised that whilst he possessed many sterling qualities, including musical ability he was somewhat disinclined to face his responsibilities on occasion, and on which in hindsight the older Fastovski now placed the blame firmly on his over-indulgence of the pie in the sky (as it were); for his somewhat excessive romanticism, and tendency towards whimsy.

This thought however was not accompanied by a blinding light on the road to Damascus, as Paul of Tarsus had experienced, and which in the latter's case had resulted in an obsessive over-dependence on either Christianity or bacon sarnies; (depending on one's point of view of course.) And whilst Fastovski was blessed with his fair share of megalomania he did not quite put himself in the same league as Paul with his fixation on converting the hitherto contented gentiles with their undoubted flair for life into that of an amended genus with rather more of an anally retentive tendency (as Fastovski suspected)…and with their feet firmly planted in the clouds, to boot. There was certainly no questioning the "grounded" qualities of the Golem's boots (a fashionable euphemism around Haverstock Hill for being "centred" or "rooted" which means the same thing really and depends basically on which yoga class one attends)…and particularly of his organic clay size sixteens which even Ray Lambert at his finest would have found a challenge to uproot. At least Fastovski had **witnessed** Ray Lambert tackles at first hand which in itself was the most grounding experience possible (but only from a safe distance) – far better than "World Music", or Psychotherapy in which the twittering classes of Hampstead appeared to indulge in a similar vein of unreality as that which Paul and his followers were afflicted…and completely unlike Paul, who had never actually *met* nor seen Jesus, nor shared some Challa, Bagels and Gefilte fish with him and his Galilean first eleven, before an away fixture at Hebron, or the big one at Jerusalem. However, like Paul he was filled with a new vision, a "raison d'etre" and a quest which in Fastovski's case, was that whilst he would leave to posterity the possibility of a shrine to Ray Lambert; he himself retained the capacity to undertake his own Lentian act of self-sacrifice, and renounce (but for good) apple pie, and all its works. Forthwith, if not sooner even!

This then was the problem that tortured Fastovski through the night and into those waking hours when man is most vulnerable to self-doubt. He had taken home some of the pie that Bartek had proffered, and had presented it to his neighbour Ulrich, who alarmingly nearly cried with ecstasy at the sight of it and which nearly prompted a sudden reversal of Fastovski's selfless gesture. But no…resolution and courage was called for here, and Fastovski stuck to his guns just like great uncle Shrolik at the siege of Port Arthur in 1904, and only would accept a single slice back in gratitude (Don't tell me that St Peter didn't don his phylacteries now and again out of romantic whimsy.) But ultimately over the next few days, he had come to the inescapable conclusion that his vacillation and other inadequacies in character were due in the main to the aforementioned dependency, and was now, finally this time, determined to give up apple pie for good. Yes, for good! He would be a new man, turn over a new leaf, make a fresh start…whatever. The problem which caused his sleeplessness however was in no way related to his giving up of the pie. No, it was all a question of honour, which Fastovski in his undoubted courtly manner exercised as a deeply held conviction. He simply was a man of his word; he hated letting people down and that next morning, he was due to collect an ***ENTIRE*** pie from Bartek which the latter had ordered for him and for which (Bartek assured him) the van was making an extra special delivery all the way from Fulham. What would Bartek think? What about the poor driver? Did he have a wife and family to support? Did Bartek know anything about phylacteries or Ray Lambert?

As the clock ticked, Fastovski sat ashen faced and immobilised by indecision and self-doubt. What could he do? He could of course say that he had changed his mind and thereby not only upset Bartek but find himself barred from the shop as a consequence. Alternatively, he could pay for the pie but decline to take it. That option, he considered, would lay him open to ridicule and he certainly did not want to become a laughing stock, to be labelled within Hampstead and Highgate, (and possibly Belsize Park and Swiss Cottage also) as great a fool as say, Til Eulenspiegl (as devotees of those mad German Richards and other lunatics might be aware). There were other fools too with whom he might stand in comparison, and much nearer to home… Oh God what a prospect. He walked to the shop with a heavy tread, a thumping heart, and an increasingly dry mouth. However he took two very deep breaths (as Mr Dodd the School Caretaker had advised him to do before his University Entrance Exams some years before, which had been good advice) and so fortified; stepped with the swaggering gait of a Polish Lancer into the shop, where Bartek was waiting for him with a big grin, and huge pie.

'God mewerning, sair,' said Bartek, greeting him affably (the Poles tend to excessive courtliness). 'The eppel pie errive hafanowerago, speshilwrap and wondairfool hafter zi cucombair sendviches end peejeeteeps weeth skeemed meelk, dont you sink?'

D Day had arrived! Fastovski mustered all the reserves of courage at his disposal, and responded in the best way he considered possible taking into account all of the aforementioned circumstances. He would be decisive, single minded, resolute and strong. 'Hello Bartek,' he breezed, 'you wouldn't care to change that there apple pie for a Teddy Bear…would you, er perhaps?'

Bartek, Pie, Fastovski

31

Murray, Ronnie, Paul and Malcolm
Fastovski waving, with "Klezmer Swingers"

Grandfather Elimelech
War veteran, 1920

Great Uncle Shrolik
Volunteer B.E.F. 1914

Fastovski (R) with pals Enna (2nd R) "Cake" (centre squatting)

Issy (with Fez) with comedians Issy Bonn (centre)

Chapter Two
Uncle Hymie

'Dey said dat **Tchaikovski** was mad…dey said dat **Napoleon** was mad…dey said dat **Louis** was mad.'

'Who's Louis?' demanded the audience.

'Louis my uncle, he *is* mad,' responded the great Schnozzle Durante (the man who found the lost chord).

Fastovski and Blueridge were chatting away amiably at Polly's Café in Hampstead, dining "al fresco", and enjoying a succulent breakfast of grilled tomatoes with garlic in olive oil, served on crisply toasted rye bread; followed by steaming pots of English Breakfast leaf tea with skimmed milk. Rashid the manic chef had served the repast in double quick time with a huge grin, and a magnificent flourish which would not have been out of place in the "Carillon" in Paris; accompanied by a laughing banter that ensued which none actually understood but which all enjoyed. Rashid hated the heat; which for an Algerian, was certainly unusual and in this he shared much in common with Fastovski with whom he spent some of his valuable time each day discussing the vicissitudes of Hampstead weather. Blueridge had already been out on the Heath that morning and loped a couple of miles, whilst Fastovski in contrast had ambled all the way from his apartment right next to the Heath and a full two minutes ambling distance from the café where he breakfasted every morning, and sometimes tea'ed also. That particular morning, he felt a little lazy and thought that he would give his pre-breakfast saunter a miss…and so bumped into his pal Blueridge who also lived in close proximity to the Heath and the café and whereas a consequence they met not infrequently. They both had a number of things in common, including successful careers in Jazz; with Blueridge enjoying an international reputation as a virtuoso jazz guitarist, and who at one time had succeeded the inestimable Django Rheinhardt as lead guitarist for the famed Stephane Grapelli…and therefore considered in the laconic nomenclature of the jazz world, as "not bad". Fastovski whilst not enjoying the same level of fame as his co-breakfaster was nevertheless recognised as an accomplished jazz pianist and with an unmatched reputation for Big Band Swing with his own Jazz Orchestra. They happened also to share a similar sense of humour with a liking for the absurd, and exercised this to the full in eclectic discussion of all manner of things in which both exhibited similar levels of passionate interest and dispassionate ennui. Both of their mothers were also ninety years old and fighting fit. Blueridge, however, for all his undoubted communicative skill, fund of knowledge and sparkling repartee was a reader of the "independent". Fastovski put this deficiency in character down to a form of savage irony, which he himself could nevertheless appreciate, and was prepared as a consequence to tolerate Blueridge's occasional fractured thinking.

That morning, the conversation had ranged from the Spanish Civil War, to the American Civil War (where they both professed the same level of knowledge and expertise)…and from the "English Civil War" where for the life of him Fastovski could discover no enthusiasm, and consequently conceded the field, as it were to Blueridge…and finally to the Commune of Paris of 1870 in which Fastovski considered himself in all modesty to be no less than the world authority, and where Blueridge considered it both prudent and expedient to make a tactical withdrawal as a consequence. Other subjects had been touched upon also to add "point and counterpoint" to the discussion, when somehow or other the conversation turned to genealogy… which possibly Blueridge had introduced…if not Fastovski…anyway it certainly wasn't Rashid who at that time was serving a table of four inside the café with further plates of all things accompanied by gesticulations and exclamations delivered in a heady mix of Pidgin English, Pidgin French, Pidgin Hampstead (and Pidgin Berber no doubt if the truth be known).

They had both been gazing appreciatively at the lovely selection of Hampstead womanhood which that morning seemed to be more in evidence than usual, when Blueridge remarked on his liking for the Oriental Woman and in particular from the Indian sub-continent. He further elaborated this with a fascinating tale of his own antecedents in the British Raj, and on which information Fastovski then made a mental note for the necessity to dissect the Indian Mutiny of 1857 next time they met. In response, Fastovski offered information of the Tatar blood which ran through the Russian Jewish veins of the Fastovski's, and of which fact he was exceedingly proud. Indeed an ex girl friend of his (and survivor from the heroic fall of the Warsaw Ghetto) had found shelter amongst the Tatars in the very village in which the young Rudolf Nureyev grew up, and when the occasion demanded Fastovski could affect both the walk and posture of Yul Brynner (again of Tatar stock) with his arms akimbo, his legs set wide, and his jaw jutting upwards. Indeed, some years before, Fastovski's infatuation with all things Russian had led him to join a London based Russian Folk dancing group composed entirely of ballet trained dancers both male and female, and which (had been) of professional standard some years prior to that. Fastovski had had no experience of the art, but the group were apparently so impressed with his swagger that he was accepted with some alacrity despite his display of uncharacteristic modesty and initial reluctance. The group practised very seriously and soon had Fastovski joining them (to his undisguised amazement) at the barre.

However, it quickly became apparent that whilst Fastovski's dramatic "Yulbrynnerisms" drew admiring comment from dancers and audiences alike it was perfectly obvious that he lacked the years and years of dedication and training necessary to accomplish the wild and difficult leg movements and contortions for which the Russian male dancers are renowned. His performances nevertheless were full of energy and style and suitable choreography was devised to exaggerate his strong points, whilst drawing attention away from his feet, knees and thighs, which were not his strong points. So much so that on one occasion a guest teacher who had danced with, and later instructed the Mariinski Ballet of Leningrad was prevailed upon to give a lesson to the group, and she immediately fell head over heels (figuratively that is) for the man who acknowledged himself as "head to waist the greatest dancer since Nijinsky, and from waist to feet, the worst dancer since Nijinsky".

Elizavetta (for that was her name) in customary manner prodded the dancers with a long stick whilst issuing exhortations and criticisms in the French/Russian argot peculiar to her trade. It soon became very obvious however that any superlatives available were directed almost shamelessly towards Fastovski; which grew increasingly obsequious and flattering as the evening went on…so much so that the other girls (one of whom he was seeing at the time) began to feel increasingly jealous and contrived somehow to form a protective wall between the two, and hastened his quick departure at the end of the class whilst themselves keeping Elizavetta engaged in conversation. Elizavetta possessed fine credentials with the Mariinsky, as well as other things too (including Fastovski's telephone number) and Fastovski will claim with some justification, that as a ballet dancer he was Mariinsky "trained". He still has his dancing boots which were made for him in the softest black leather in Moscow and where presumably the boot last is still stored. Probably next to Yul's.

Naturally, none of this more intimate information had been relayed to Blueridge, and anyhow Blueridge by now was negotiating a fruit salad with one of the waitresses, and Fastovski felt that Blueridge's attentions (quite rightly) were on the composition of grape, mango, orange, star fruit, red and white berry, Chinese gooseberry, physalis and white peach in which he was now tucking into with undisguised gusto and only moderate expense.

What you may ask, has this to do with mad uncle Hymie; or with Schnozzle Durante?

Well, the point is that whilst Schnozzle's uncle was perhaps apocryphal, Fastovski's was the real thing and most certainly was mad. More strictly he was a cousin of his father Issy and had hailed from the vicinity of Fastovski only two thousand *versts* from Moscow (as Gogol would have put it) and from where his side of the family drew its name. In appearance Hymie was as distinctive and unusual as indeed was Schnozzle in his own way, but at that point any further resemblance ceased. Hymie was somewhat startling to behold and even more startling to speak to (if you either possessed the courage, or were availed of no other option) He possessed the stocky Fastovski build, was of medium height and sported a Russian style "kartoshka" (potato nose) somewhat like Kruschev's in proportion, but exhibiting a distinctive and remarkable shade of purple. This was framed by huge white eyebrows which almost completely concealed his eyes, and which themselves almost met his hairline (giving him the appearance of Lawrence Talbot aka "The Wolf Man") His crowning glory was a mass of frizzy unrestrained white hair which stuck out on both sides of his head very much in the style of Ben Gurion, first Prime Minister of Israel. Hymie was never known to smile, and addressed everybody in the same slow Lancashire burr of Blackburn where he landed up with some of the family as refugees towards the end of the Russian Civil War…(which reminds me; on that subject Fastovski and Blueridge had both "retired with honour"…scale too vast…issues too complex…sundry Fastovskis popping up all over the place)… His gait was very slow and deliberate and was occasioned by some problem with his feet the cause of which was never really known. Hymie had actually told a very young and somewhat enraptured Fastovski that he (Hymie, that is) had been born with his feet back to front and which had been turned around by a doctor in Blackpool. The only reason that his mother had arranged this, he explained, was because he kept falling down the stairs.

Such infirmity and other lack of social grace did not, it transpired inhibit his success with the ladies, and was eventually referred to by friend and enemy alike as "Bluebeard" which at that time indicated multi-marriages and naughty goings on in the intervals between. He had been married a number of times it is true, but how many; nobody knew for certain. His current wife however was a Dutch lady of sinisterly spiteful appearance and with whom he seemed to get along with very well and with whom he shared a rather nice Edwardian house in a leafy area of Southport near the Victorian arcade-rich magnificence of Lord Street...the finest street in the Kingdom no doubt. Fastovski's grandparents also lived in Southport, and with whom Hymie enjoyed a good relationship. The grandmother "Anna" (the Russianised form of "Nehama", her Hebrew name meaning "Revenge"), and normally expressed in the Russian/Jewish diminuitive as "Nechamka" by which she was generally known; was occasionally to be found in the cafés in Lord Street, together with an entire colony of Russian Jewish "Bobbischkes" (many widowed from the civil war) and chatting away in Yiddish. Nechamka, however, spoke (and wrote) Russian fluently so somewhere she had received a "Russian" education which for a Jewish girl in the early 1880s was usually not to be obtained. Sitting amongst the group and chatting away merrily was a lady called Mrs Kerensky who happened to be the widow of Kerensky himself, the President of the Duma and first minister of Social Democratic Russia at the time of the Revolution of

1917 and before his overthrow by Lenin and their subsequent flight. In order to achieve anonymity, Kerensky was obliged to disguise himself as a woman, and, so the story goes, because of his slim and elegant posture and rather pretty face looked even more strikingly beautiful than the attractive Mrs Kerensky, and more fashionably dressed. Strange juxtaposition of fate. Neither Mrs Kerensky (nor indeed) her husband were Jewish, but Mrs Kerensky assimilated herself happily into the Yiddish/Russian speaking circle of "Bobbischkes" in the lovely town of Southport and in time became indistinguishable from her emigre friends. They were all, after all Russians.

Nechamka's husband "Elimelech" translated roughly as "God the King" in the beautiful and poetic Hebrew; spent most of his time in his tailoring workshop in the front room of the terrace house which they shared in a nice quiet respectable area, and where blazened on the walls were photographs of the great Russian Generals and leaders From Stalin, to Zhukov, Timoshenko and many, many more. In his younger days, he too had been a lothario of some repute, and unlike the hirsute Hymie was extremely handsome in a "lounge lizard" sort of way, and was over six feet tall with blond hair and smiling blue eyes. It was said that women would swoon at the very sight of him. He was a regular supporter of Southport F.C (The "Sangrounders" they were called) where he was to be found every Saturday afternoon having earlier returned from morning service at the little synagogue at Arnside Road…and, after dining off the chicken soup with kneidlach, chopped liver, roast chicken with roast potatoes, red cabbage and "Tzimmes" (a sweet accompaniment of carrot, flour and farfel) followed by lokshen pudding and lemon tea drunk Russian style direct from the burnished copper Samovar that stood proudly on the burnished mahogany sideboard into small glasses then breaking by hand the hard chunks of pure white sugar and into the mouth to receive the amber nectar all of which Nechamka had prepared entirely by herself as any good Jewish woman would and without complaining more than absolutely necessary. *(All true, but with an apology to Isaac Babel!)*

Elimelech, (referred to by his young and only grandson, as "Zeider") and like the entire breed of Russian Jews given sanctuary in the UK was fanatically patriotic and did not limit his martial fervour to photographs of Russian Generals. He had been mustard gassed on the Western Front in 1915, but he had somehow or other been accepted into the RAF in some capacity or other soon after war broke out again in 1939, and young Fastovski was filled with pride at the sight of this aged but vigorous and upright colossus striding evenly towards him down the street like a God (which indeed he was by name, of course) in the wonderful RAF blue uniform complemented by his strong and shining blue eyes. A photograph still exists of him taken in the uniform at the time.

'Hot Water?' Blueridge and Fastovski had finished their breakfast almost simultaneously; timing which would have been calamitous in a jazz gig at Ronnie Scotts, but was nevertheless quite acceptable in a more "rubato a la tomato" environment... 'Hot water?' The question was articulated at the two companions by the magnificent Pam, who whilst not the owner of the said café nevertheless was its hub, its core and around who's ample bosom everything revolved. Pam was (and still is of course) a very personable and attractive lady not exactly in her first flush of youth (as she would not mind admitting) friendly, warm, open and also very humorous in a somewhat self-effacing way…and full of bubbly charm. In fact her attractive appearance and demeanour was a heady combination of "Glamourpuss" and "School Matron" and with a certain resemblance to Purity Pinker (as some of you might remember, the long-time companion and would-be amour of Robert Newton aka Long John Silver the renowned charlatan, rogue, freebooter and pirate)…a gentleman who would no doubt have fitted in quite nicely in Hampstead; provided of course that he occasionally read the "Guardian". To add to the imagery of the said Purity Pinker, Pam and her husband actually had ownership of some land on a small uninhabited island in the West Indies. On receipt of this revelation, Fastovski's imaginative processes whooshed into overdrive; with visions of Pam (Purity) serving Long John Blueridge with copious drafts of rum, surrounded by his scurvy crew of "dogs" "curs" "jazz musicians" and such like in her tavern "The Bucket of Blood" on her treasure Island, deep in the Spanish Main, or indeed in the café in Hampstead… Blueridge on observing that Fastovski was in the throes of self-induced poetic reverie, accepted Pam's kind offer and both tea pots were replenished forthwith.

'Hot Water? What do you mean…hot water," said Morton, first cousin to Hymie, and a man who at the age of sixty had suddenly discovered to his delight that (to his own considered opinion, and everybody else's dismay) he had been blessed with hitherto unrevealed artistic ability and had decamped to St Ives in Cornwall and busied himself for the next two years in blissful creativity of seascapes, landscapes and foodscapes with a pronounced leaning to a sort of crazed, drunken, drugged and retarded Jackson Pollock style of canvas desecration. Morton, however, considered that they combined the mysticism of Chagall, the geometrical symbiosis of Braque leavened with the inverse pigmentation of Kandinsky all put together in an environment of Daliesque surrealism. In short, they were absolutely awful…a sort of painting in fact for people who hated paintings…and probably that's the kindest thing that could be said for the efforts of the kindly ever beaming friendly and inoffensive gentleman…a sort of Pickwick amongst painters.

Morton was particularly busy that morning and had been standing back and admiring his latest masterpiece which combined a sewing machine, flying Jew and fishing smack; when he was somewhat wrong footed by an insistent ringing of the telephone which, disturbing his reverie, he answered in an uncharacteristic manner of some tetchiness to be advised that his mother the famed Mrs Schwartzwald who had passed her driving test on her first attempt at the age of eighty six had yet again been arrested by the police when found in the act of cutting telephone wires at the top of a telephone pole after having received previous assurances from her family and indeed from the good lady herself that she would not under any circumstances do this again and would not require psychiatric treatment. It all ran in the family, you see.

A little after this episode, Fastovski and his parents were discussing the aforementioned events whilst not enjoying afternoon tea together with some assorted strange persons with Hymie and his sinister spouse. Hushed tones were the order of the day at such gatherings, primarily because of general fear of upsetting Hymie for any reason which might take his fancy, or indeed which might not. Fastovski's father Issy (the gentleman's barber, Yiddish humourist and showman) also enjoyed a similar reputation to Hymie, devoid however of the rampant insanity with which Hymie had been blessed...in other words, he was for all his formidable reputation for outlandish behaviour, not in the same league as his cousin. Issy was a fanatical boxing enthusiast whose heroes included Jack Dempsey (The Manasseh Mauler), Max Baer (the Jewish heavyweight trained by Dempsey) and a puncher of such deadly power that he had killed two men in the ring...he afterwards always pulled his punches and clowned his way through to numerous victories, and some defeats. He also rated amongst his heroes his Liverpool pal and middleweight Nel Tarleton, and the London based Jewish boxers Jack (Kid) Berg and Ted (Kid) Lewis...all world champions. This is mentioned solely to place the startling unpredictability factor in relationship of Issy to Hymie in boxing terms, which Issy would certainly appreciate and endorse. Hymie however would not appreciate and most certainly not understand virtually anything. You see, if Hymie could be considered the Jack Dempsey of "Mishagas" (a form of benign hyperactive insanity...as the Yiddishists would describe it) then Issy by comparison could only enjoy identification with "Slappsy Maxie" Rosenbloom...a great broken-nosed fighter certainly, but of much less fearsome reputation.

Perhaps, Hymie had overheard the mention of his Auntie Schwartzwald (his hearing was indeed very acute), but for whatever reason it triggered the awaited episode of inspired madness in which on every possible occasion he subjected his visitors…the dreaded group photograph. He ordered everybody out, which the group complied with some alacrity and faces filled with fear with Issy in the vanguard; possibly in the belief that the rear-guard posed the most danger due to its proximity to Hymie who was still drinking his tea and eating his Marie biscuit; slowly and carefully. The group milled outside in some confusion and trepidation for a couple of minutes when Hymie appearing with a Leica camera and wiping the crumbs from his mouth and carefully blowing his magnificent blue nose into a huge carefully pressed white handkerchief stood there in the sunshine with his knotted tie wrapped loosely around his much-too-large stiff collar with the shirt sleeves of his faded mustard coloured check shirt rolled up around his weighty arms and his shapeless heavy woollen dun-green trousers lying somewhere on his chest whilst suspended in a pair of scarlet braces…on his feet he wore his customary highly polished brown reinforced boots, and on 'is 'ead, 'e were wearin' 'is flat 'at.

A deadly hush descended on the multitude which for the next twenty minutes or so were barked into different groupings, postures and poses with Issy especially being singled out for the most Peripatetic reorientation and all behaving with total submissiveness and compliance. No refusal, no rebellion, no dissent. On conclusion of the photographic session which had been accompanied by knowing glances between the braver hearts present, and with actual much enjoyment by the young Fastovski, Hymie announced in his deadpan Lancashire monotone that he had now finished "tekkin" the photographs and that he had not put a film in the camera (as indeed he never did and of which they were all well aware) and barked everybody back to the table to continue their tea and Marie Biscuit as if nothing had happened.

Fastovski (aged 20 with L.S.E. tie!)

Issy on SS "Dorsetshire"

Chapter Three
Issy Is or Issy Ain't

The Stag Night

'Cor Blimey…what a conk! Anybody would fink I was a
Jew!' The gentleman who uttered this reflection on the
Jewish physiognomy was not himself Jewish (as could be
ascertained) but was indeed the possessor of a
magnificent hooter which would have put in the shade the
infamous and foul portrayal of "Jewishness" by "Sir"

Alec Guinness in the film "Oliver Twist" in 1948. The young Fastovski had seen this film when on holiday in Blackpool with his parents on a black rainy night, and was caught up in the gasp of horror from the audience at the portrayal of Fagin in a manner which did credit to the Nazi propaganda films of very recent memory, when "the Jew" was portrayed as degenerate, loathsome…and fitting only for annihilation.

Definitely, a case of "a bridge too far". The gentleman who offered the observation however was not intending to be unfriendly but was somehow attempting (misguidedly it quickly became apparent) to ingratiate himself with the audience for which he had been booked to entertain. The gentleman in question was the film actor/comedian Ronald Shiner who on the strength of some quickfire cockney argot allied to a nose of heroic proportion (and little else by way of talent it seems) was fortunate in being able to create a career of some fame and merciful short duration. The problem was (for him) that the audience to whom the remark was addressed was comprised entirely of Liverpool Jewish ex-serviceman out for a stag night (maybe his agent didn't like him and didn't tell him). One or two of the audience in the dark smoky hall that evening certainly displayed more than the usual entitlement of nose, but they were outnumbered by others of a more "broken nose variety" who began to mutter darkly as Shiner (having by now realised his faux pas) was, with increasing red faced desperation attempting to extricate himself by relaying further "Jewish jokes" (he did not possess the wit to try Irish or Scottish).

However, the damage was irretrievable, and soon the poor unfortunate was looking nervously to the side of the stage, as the muttering grew in some intensity (accompanied by friendlier chants of "Bring on the Stripper") which prevailed upon the elephant man to withdraw timidly, with a sickly grin, to thunderous silence, as the trio struck up a raunchy number. This naturally pacified the audience and hastened the appearance of the stripper, and the retreat of the oleaginous oaf, who disappeared from view in a miasmic haze of bay rum hair oil, and the sweat of fear. Serves him right!

In consort with his chums, Issy was annoyed not only at the crude jibe of the aforementioned miscreant, but also at the unprofessional standard of his performance. You see; Issy was a showman; a performer, one of best MCs in the business, confidant of some of the big names in showbiz, and responsible for giving local talent their "first break". Into this latter category such names spring to mind as Jimmy Tarbuck, Johnny Hackett, and Michael Holliday (who sang like Bing Crosby) and who later died in some suspicious circumstances at the Freddie Mills Club off Tottenham Court Road; where Mills (and boxing hero of Issy) was himself killed in a gangland execution a year or so later, and in the manner of the Jewish Gangsters; by being shot through the eyes; as was Buggsy Siegel. Issy was an intuitive comedian and compere, and probably the best Yiddishist on the stage in the business – to be compared only with Jackie Mason (some years later) for sheer inventiveness, charisma and chutzpah. Strolling troubadours, the talented and untalented of every form of artistic endeavour including clowns, comedians, contortionists, ventriloquists, crooners, opera singers and plain idiots baked the trail to Issy's Barber Shop on Brownlow Hill ("Is" is a whizz with the scizz…English spoken!) where he would not only cut hair and shave the customers but engage in never ending banter; mainly one sided. For those customers of a more insular disposition Issy employed "Ronnie the Silent Barber". At around this time, Issy had been approached by a travelling Yiddish Theatre Company from London which comprised the Principal (a rather fat and pompous elderly tragedian of "the Old School" which at that time was rapidly dying out)…accompanied by a young tall and very attractive blond "assistant"…and which in total, constituted the Theatre Company in its entirety. The performance was devised as a monologue with selected speeches from Shylock ("Hath not a Jew eyes…") and from the Yiddish writings of Scholem Aleichem, Mendele Moykher-Sforim; Peretz and Ansky; whilst the "assistant" confined her activities presumably to off-stage and other requirements. The great actor wanted Issy to promote the show, to which he assented. The entire Theatre Company was accommodated in a double room in a cheap hotel behind Lime Street Station, and in a matter of two weeks Issy had provided a sold out performance at the Picton Hall, (where a year or two later young Fastovski would see in concert the great jazz pianist Teddy Wilson; from America; accompanied by Dick the one eyed drummer from Liverpool, on loan from the Merseysippi Jazz Band…) Issy introduced the great Yiddish actor who initially was received with somewhat respectful but muted applause to be succeeded after a short while by shuffling, scratching, and some talking, and with the onset at twenty minutes or so of the same dark mutterings that had characterised the demise of the other actor from London at the said stag night. Issy being the showman he was, had done his job only too well. He certainly had not misrepresented the nature of the performance to the public; as he worked to high standards of professional integrity, but his energetic enthusiasm was as contagious as an invasion of Salt Beef into Stepney, and there was indeed a veritable clamour for the tickets. The great tragedian somehow blustered his over-dramatic and hopelessly old-fashioned way through to the interval, accompanied by increasing sighs and groans from the audience and, bowing backwards (as he probably imagined did Sir Henry Irving at Drury Lane, in his prime) made his exit to a deep sigh of relief from the audience accompanied by a hasty departure by some hundreds from their ranks scrambling and trampling over each other in desperation to escape.

Issy, who was sitting in the audience with his wife Tilly and young Fastovski (their sole offspring) was perhaps for the only time in his life…absolutely speechless. Prior to his introducing the act which he did with both the appropriate degree of gravitas (as the occasion demanded) and with commendable brevity; he had ensured that he donned full stage make up for the occasion, complete with powder, mascara, eye liner and rouged cheeks, and lipstick…which however he had omitted to remove prior to joining his wife and child in the audience and consequently drew astonished looks from the Children of Israel in their exodus from the Picton Hall. Issy was a "doppelganger" of Akim Tamiroff the film actor and of Charlie Cairoli, the great Clown and Showman resident for years and years at the "Tower", Blackpool.

His transmogrification into a combination of the two at such a dramatic juncture, (allied to a suggestion of dubious sexual orientation) added to the overall atmosphere of panic and surrealism which would assuredly have even eluded Morton the artist in the fastnesses of St Ives (and not far incidentally from the village of St Issy…would you believe).

The remainder of the audience however retained their seats, probably out of some sense of loyalty to Issy (or more probably because they had no homes to go to) and awaited for the second half…and waited…and waited. Soon (being a Liverpool audience) the barracking started preceded by a rising crescendo of slow handclapping, which culminated in the usual Yiddo-Scouse witticisms of an anarchic and disrespectful nature. Eventually, the blonde appeared on the stage and appealed for a doctor as the actor had taken ill.

Issy (and young Fastovski in his wake), dashed backstage to find the poor man in great discomfort (a mild heart attack, from which he did recover) and mercifully not comatose; seated and being examined by Doctor Braslavsky who had responded very quickly. A quick conference was held and Issy agreed that (rather than cancel the event), he himself would do the second half. Without script or preparation, he ad-libbed his way through forty five minutes of superb spontaneous Yiddish humour…and by common consent a complete "tour de force"…

The next day, he went back to being a barber.

That generation of Liverpool Jews to which Issy belonged were either immigrants from Russia (mainly Odessa and the Ukraine hinterland) or the children of immigrants. They loved their adopted country with a passion, and brought into it all the joy, energy and bawdy rough-hewn humour so typical of the Russian Jews... "The jolly fat Jews of the South" as Isaac Babel the Jewish-Odessan author and Cossack Cavalryman described them. Back home in "Russland", they had received little or no schooling, were excluded from most trades and professions, and were subjected to forced conscription into the Russian Army; being obliged to serve a term of twenty-five years.

Despite their providing a very high proportion at any time of seasoned professional soldiers, they were denied commission into the officer class. Shrolik Fastovski (Issy's uncle who as a child had rummaged in the dustbins to obtain food scraps for his family during the pogrom in Elizavetgrad in 1881) had served as an artilleryman at Vladivostock in 1904 in the Russo-Japanese war, and later enlisted in the British Army in 1914. Issy's father Elimelech; similarly had been an infantryman in the Imperial Russian Army; had later enlisted in the British Army in 1914 and was invalided out in 1915 after being mustard gassed in the trenches of Ypres on the Western Front. Issy's wife Tilly had two uncles who served as Cavalrymen with the Red Cossacks (one of whom was called "Burl",) and were killed during the Russian Civil War. It is a strange irony that the Cossack Cavalry training centre was based in Elizavetgrad, the home of the "other side" of Fastovski's grandparents, who as related by Issy had supported the White Russian Army, and may possibly have fought in its ranks alongside thousands of other Jews loyal to the Social Democratic government of Kerensky which had been overthrown by the Bolsheviks. Not all Jews were Bolsheviks. Others fought in the Ranks of the Ukrainian Army under Petlurya, and large numbers under the charismatic and romantic Makhnov, with his anarchist anti-communist peasant and workers army. The third brother (possibly called Morris) survived the war but was probably shot at Ponary near Riga by the Germans in 1943 together with some 80,000 fellow Latvian Jews, including Tilly's entire family. Tilly's father Wolf ("Velvel" in the Yiddish) a Latvian immigrant, enlisted in the Royal Welsh Fusiliers on the outbreak of the First World War. He later transferred to the 38th battalion of the Royal London Fusiliers comprising six hundred London based Russian Jews which fought in the Palestine campaign under General Allenby. Fastovski had never met his "Zeider Wolf" as he had died in 1930 of Tuberculosis. When Tilly passed away aged 99 in 2013, Fastovski found a bundle of letters from her soldier brother Morris who had been killed just before the end of World War Two near Dusseldorf. In his honour and for his memory, Fastovski has compiled in book form the letters together with a commentary on the Brown and Feldman Families who created the backdrop to the short and heroic life of his uncle who he remembers with love and admiration after all these years. The book is called "Letters from a Soldier" now in archive in The Imperial War Museum, Kennington, London.

Fastovski considered his uncle Connie "Buster" Harris from Leeds as somewhat of an icon…indeed as were all the members of this family of strong independent and brave men whose names will provide the glow of pride to their descendent families. Look-alike of Clark Gable "The King of Hollywood", Connie liked the ladies. Quiet, mildly ironic, with an infectious laugh and superbly engaging "naughty boy" personality. Tall and broad shouldered, he made his living as a croupier and played Rugby at weekends around Yorkshire where he was considered to be of County Standard. He never made an enemy in his life. On the outbreak of war in 1939, Connie was "on the town" with some of his pals, much the worse for wear with drink when the three decided that they might just as well volunteer for the RAF, as the pubs were shut (He loved his "Tetleys Yorkshire Ale"). His mother Baila was not too pleased. Connie was shipped out to Singapore where for the next two years he enjoyed the social life around Raffles Hotel, the company of the officer's wives and his selection into the United Services Rugby team which included some International standard players. As the Japanese were advancing on Singapore, much of the garrison was being evacuated either back to "Blighty" or to India. Connie, however, was having such a good time, and wishing to remain around Raffles Hotel…cocktails, ladies and gambling…that (as he put it) he "pulled a few strings" and was transferred to another unit which was scheduled to remain. Caught up in the ensuing debacle, he was captured with his whole unit, transferred to a prison ship and secreted in the hold with hundreds of others and transferred to a P.O.W. camp in Japan. Later when Connie would relate stories of his capture and incarceration in the camp, he would never ever speak of what happened in the dreadful hold of that ship. From 1941 until Japan's capitulation in 1945, he managed to survive the barbaric conditions in the camp in circumstances of near-starvation and constant beatings…whilst fulfilling his use as a slave labourer in the mines and at the nearby dockyard of Kobe. Most of his colleagues succumbed either to the brutality, starvation or cholera and dysentery which were endemic in the camp.

One touch of humanity which the Japanese allowed was the provision of a dog eared "Complete and unabridged works of Shakespeare" and "The Bible". Connie learned the entire content of both by heart and at ninety-five, he seemed little the worse for wear for that dreadful experience of which he and only a handful of his compatriots survived. 'It were summat that 'appened,' he would say when asked for the secret of his survival. Accept life and get on with it…a philosophy which in many ways seemed to convey the spirit of The Fastovski, The Feldman, The Braun, The Greengut, The Harris, in the best Jewish way. For Connie like all the best Jews, their Jewishness is carried lightly and in Connie's case on a par with his being a Yorkshireman. 'I were best croupier in Yorkshire,' Connie would say and his niece Sonya in deepest Halifax would advise that when he says "Best in Yorkshire" that it should be construed as "Best in't World".

One morning before roll call in the camp, the inmates were awoken by a ferocious explosion in the distance which sounded like the End of the Earth. The guards noticeably omitted their brutality and a few days later seemed to melt away. The camp thirty miles from Hiroshima was secured by the "Yanks" and Connie was sent to recuperate for six months in a military hospital in Australia, and for part of the time as the guest of a lovely family. On enlistment, the burly Yorkshireman had weighed over thirteen stone and on release a little above six; having survived on a diet mainly on rice with a little seaweed. On his return to Leeds, Baila greeted him with a "nice rice pudding". He ate every bit. No word or expression of bitterness or regret ever escaped his lips either about his experiences or about the Japanese. Indeed, he spoke the language reasonably well and until the end at the age of 96 would refer to his mythical Geisha girlfriend (who he kept "upstairs") as "Ice Cream" (I SCREAM!)...

Sonya found among his belongings wrapped in a towel in the wardrobe, two large and thick diaries written by Connie whilst a POW. She only had time to glance through them before returning home. Leaving the car for a brief time to pick up something from a shop, she returned to find her brief case in which she had placed the diaries had been stolen from the unlocked car.

Connie would always drop into the Fastovskis for the Grand National at Aintree, sometimes to stay. Issy always seemed to hold "open house" often to the consternation of Tilly who would be obliged on occasion to provide shelter for some dubious new acquaintance of her husband who likely as not would eventually swindle him out of some money, sometimes of a considerable amount. Issy in his quest for acceptance would leave himself open to the unscrupulous who would take advantage of him time and time again. In that regard, he let his family down badly, and sadly was unapproachable on the subject. For the whole of his life, he lacked a sense of security and (like many comedians) was somewhat of a Pagliacci. He surrounded himself with Damon Runyonesque characters who were often to be found at the house dining well on his diminishing resources, but who nevertheless were extremely entertaining and brilliant personalities, in their own way. They all enjoyed a nickname culture in imitation of the Jewish Gangsters of New York, Lower East side. Issy was known as "Issy the Greek" both for his appearance, his friendship with the Greeks and his facility with the language which he spoke "Sailor style". Dave Rosenberg was known as "Docker" for some shady goings on in his sphere of operations, the vast network of the Liverpool docks. Louis Rogansky was known as "The Rajah" which was out by his Indian appearance, suitably imperious manner and his unaccountable sumptuous lifestyle. Mick Lesin was known as "Big Mick" simply borne due to his towering presence with a face somewhat like Freddy Mills the boxer and was owner of the Night Club "Ace of Spades". The imposing and mysterious Joey Graff lived in a suite in the grand Adelphi Hotel; where Issy would come on demand to shave him in oil and essences in the fashion of the New York Jewish Gangsters. Fastovski was honoured to accompany his father on one occasion to visit the great man who spoke very quietly and in who's presence Issy was entirely deferential and never uttered a single joke. Sometime later Issy bought a huge ferocious full-grown Tabby Cat for his son as a present; which was the "King of the Block", terrorising cats and dogs alike, but otherwise lying quietly on the couch and eschewing attention and affection. Fastovski named him "Joey Graff". One gentleman referred to as "Louis the Chink" again for reasons of tincture and physiognomy, and possibly with something or other also to do with Chinatown (Mein Gott the Jews are a diverse lot). Tevya Chernyshevsky was the one that young Fastovski enjoyed listening to above all. A forebear had apparently been publicly pilloried in the main square of St Petersburg in 1864 for his sarcastic condemnation of the czar, and Tevya with his wit, intelligence and quick-fire Yiddish, which could at times match Issy the Master; would enthral the young boy. His seemingly endless ability to express joyful unremitting hatred for absolutely everybody, for any particular reason, and in such fine style, was a marvel to behold. He was the Jack Buchanan of elegant intolerance. It is worth mentioning here that one of Fastovski's pals would boast that his grandfather was the very first man in the whole of Russia to be run over and killed by an automobile; Packard most likely. A most amusing anecdote which was repeated on occasions by the eponymous gentlemen; related to an episode during the war when a merchant ship in which both "Docker" and "Rajah" were serving was torpedoed just off Aden. Each of the two swore that on swimming towards the shore, he had heard some splashing distance away, the Jewish prayer on dying, accompanied by some gurgling and swearing, and thereupon gave rescue to his drowning friend. To this day, nobody knows for sure who was telling the truth, but it really doesn't matter.

Connie "Buster" Harris RAF 1939

**Alderman Edwin Marshall Clein Lord Mayor of Liverpool
2000 (AKA Marshal Klein)**

Issy and his cronies were all snappy dressers, and wore the best tailor-made suits, silk shirts and ties, and "gangster-style" trilbies. They all effected the tough Liverpool argot which at that time was delivered very clearly, very directly with a beautiful "line" spoken hard through the top teeth which would stay revealed during discourse (very like the Humphrey Bogart manner of delivery) and very unlike the current degraded "Scouse" spoken today by the younger generation with its pitiful lilting effeminate whine. They walked with the rolling gait of the Liverpool Sailors (which indeed most of them were) which in "Old Liverpool" were known as a "Dicky Sam". They were courteous, kind, funny and would stand no nonsense.

Issy got on very well with Ralph, Fastovski's eventual father-in-law. Like Issy, Ralph was of Russian stock, and an excellent Yiddishist, but unlike Issy, a man who would not court publicity. They shared a liking for "the noble art" and Ralph was pally with a lot of the London Jewish Boxers, some of whom would visit him at home. He himself had in his younger days, been a very good wrestler, and had been in street fights against the Blackshirts in London's East End before the war, as had Issy in Liverpool (and also in the merchant navy in which he had later served). On the outbreak of war in 1939 Ralph had joined the fire service (he was passed unfit for military service due to an ulcer), and saw dreadful things during the London blitz in 1940. This was accomplished at the expense of his thriving tailoring business which he neglected and for which his wife never forgave him. Issy had not been eligible for military service due to his Russian Nationality and had joined the Home

Guard where he was assigned to an anti-aircraft regiment with gun emplacements in Sefton Park. During the entire course of the Blitz in which vast acres of the docks and City centre were totally destroyed and thousands killed, his unit was not credited with a single hit against the Heinkel and Dornier Bombers which were circling over Liverpool like vultures. Issy maintained that the level of expertise amongst his fellow gunners was such that they were incapable even of hitting the sky. In sheer desperation the War Office sent some top secret experimental rockets (and two very tough Cockney Sergeants according to Issy) which again failed to effect a single hit. The Rockets as such were retired from service thereafter as were Home Guard Israel Feldman and the rest of the Unit. He worked also for the Yankee Officers in Liverpool and was rewarded with huge tips and not-to-be-obtained wartime luxuries such as bananas, sweets and chocolates and tough pink bubble gum. He later squandered his geldt on the gee-gees and never owned a car nor indeed his own house. Ralph managed both but lived (with his wife) in constant debt and great unhappiness in his later years. Whilst a student at the L.S.E, Fastovski fulfilled the role of courier between Issy and Ralph in their respective cities and relaying long chat/monologues/jokes in Yiddish to which each would respond in their own particular way. The messages had been recorded on the Grundig reel to reel tape recorder which weighed fifty pounds (Fastovski was quite happy to lug the huge machine between London and Liverpool): and which his parents had bought for him at "Nems" the famous music shop run by Brian Epstein, a little while before he took over the Beatles. On his return visits to Liverpool during his University years, Fastovski was often to be found playing jazz piano at the "Blue Angel" which was owned by Alun Williams (the then manager of the Beatles): and an establishment where all the musicians, poets, and literati mingled in the vibrant Bohemian atmosphere which has always permeated Liverpool society. Ralph did not have a happy marriage, and when he died from a massive heart attack some years later; Issy, the uneducated brash showman, and avid reader of Keats, Coleridge and John Donne, cried like a child.

Like Issy, Ralph was not in the slightest regard a timid man; nor would he have felt overawed by anybody…until he met Hymie that is. It happened this way. Hymie was aware that young Fastovski and spouse were to visit Liverpool and sent him a letter requesting he purchase certain items for him in London; written no doubt in the flat Lancashire accent in which he uttered any pronouncement, and to whom, and for what. Thus, 'Listen Velvel, (the diminutive by which young Fastovski was often addressed) I want you to get for me some things I 'ave ordered in Lunden. What I want is the following one-and-a-half- pounds of Jewish biscuits from the Jewish shop at 1/9d per lb and a cock new 'atched canary yellow Dutch tell me when you're arriving, Uncle Hymie'

Fastovski kept the letter but sadly it has now been lost.

The details as to where the items had been ordered where omitted as presumably he considered either that London possessed only a sole purveyor of "Jewish" biscuits, and solitary dealer in "new 'atched"…(and in which case Fastovski would be aware of this), or more likely still; he didn't consider it necessary that young

Velvel Fastovski should be made aware at all. This certainly would have been consistent with the modus operandi he employed in getting everybody to run around for him, and in particular Issy; who nevertheless was as helpless as a moth in Hymie's flame of insane genius which was of Olympian stature, at the very least… Fastovski nevertheless considered it expedient to telephone Hymie to gather such information as necessary in order to facilitate his instructions. It transpired that he had not actually ordered the items, and agreed to leave the actual brand of biscuit to the discretion of the young man in consultation with the shopkeeper. He was also allowed some latitude in the price of 1/9d per lb with some initial reluctance, and provided he secured a receipt. He offered no information at all on the whereabouts of the "new 'atched canary" nor it's selling price and on that basis, he seemed quite content to let Fastovski sort the matter out for him. The bird (together with transporter cage) were conveyed (together with the Jewish biscuits…and Fastovski's wife) by car (Ford E93A) directly to Southport. A slight moment of panic had ensued during the journey when the canary escaped captivity and flew around the car but was enticed back and received his reward of being baptised in the name of Cedric. Hymie expressed his approval of the name, the canary and the biscuits, but told Fastovski (quite mildly) that the bird was not in fact "new 'atched". It was only after returning to London that he learned from Hymie that the "new 'atched Cock" was in fact a hen. Hymie delivered the information in a matter of fact tone and told the young man that he still called the re-gendered avian "Cedric".

Hymie had always entertained a liking for the young Fastovski and had always spoken to him kindly and indeed with some obvious respect...and it was probably for this reason that he allowed actual discussion of his dictats and demands. Issy was most impressed and acknowledged that such latitude from the dreaded Hymie would most certainly not have come his own way in like circumstance; or in fact under any circumstances whatsoever.

When Hymie was in an advanced stage of cirrhosis of the liver, he was referred by Southport General Hospital to the National Liver Hospital at Gray's Inn Road London. Fastovski and wife visited him regularly and undertook such errands as he might require. However, on that occasion when Fastovski brought Ralph to visit the "Bluebeard with the Blue nose", the said gentleman had now accrued a most vivid yellow ochre which overall gave his face a distinct resemblance to the flag of Sweden. Hymie was wary of Ralph, and one could detect some anxiety building up in Ralph; who in order to help Hymie and more likely still, to make himself acceptable to the strange Lancastrian; fell into a trap entirely of his own devising and for which he was to suffer the ultimate penalty.

'Is there anything I can get you Hymie?' said Ralph, in his gruff but pleasant cockney.

'Aye...there is,' said Hymie... 'Get me some of that...grey... stuff... you get from Jewish Shops.'

'Do you mean chopped herring,' said Ralph.

'Naw...' responded Hymie, a little tetchily.

'Er...gefilte fish then,' suggested Ralph.

'*NAW… THAT'S NOT GREY STUFF,*' exclaimed Hymie, with increasing irritation, and in a voice heard right throughout the ward.

'Er… well… err… perhaps shmaltz herring… or err… gafelbitter,' offered poor Ralph who by now was well impaled Issy style; on the deadly hook of Hymie, the Torquemada of the North.

'***NAWWWWW… I WANT GREARRR STUFF… AND NOWT ELSE,*** shouted Hymie, to the mixed amusement and horror of the bedridden audience and visitors**.

Mrs Fastovski whispered to Ralph that he perhaps should try "Halvah", which Ralph did, and which appeared to pacify the angry sandgrounder… 'Aye,' he responded… 'Alver…that's it…get me some…alver…'

The following evening, after sweating all day in the death throes of his once thriving tailoring factory, Ralph was picked up by Fastovski in order to visit Hymie. He confided to his son-in-law that he had had no time to visit a Jewish shop in order to acquire the appropriate "grey stuff" for the demanding liver patient, but had obtained what appeared to be a catering size pack of a Greek alternative (complete with the peculiar form of non-Lancastrian hieroglyphics to which the Greeks are prone) and which he assumed would be suitable.

Fastovski realising that Ralph had not had a particularly good day, kept his misgivings on that subject to himself.

'Hello, Hymie,' said the amiable Ralph…

'Elaw…' responded Hymie with the usual benign antipathy he seemed to display for everybody save Fastovski, and his own sour-pussed Dutch wife.

'Here you are, Hymie,' said Ralph, 'I've brought you some halvah.' Handing the near suitcase size packet of Greek paste to the fearsome one.

'What's all this?' said Hymie, without the merest expression of gratitude; whilst turning the packet over and examining the baffling sylliric which bore no relation to the ancient scriptures of Israel which Hymie had been anticipating, nor indeed of anything which otherwise might be understood in Rawtenstall, Ramsbottom, Heckmondwike or indeed anywhere else in Lancashire.

'It's… er… halvah… Hymie…Greek Halvah; I'm sure you'll like it.' Gulped the once proud East End gentleman who was now being reduced with increasing rapidity to the status of shimmering protoplasm.

'Aye… dawnt… wunt… ***Bloody GREEK alver,***' shouted Hymie to a now panic-stricken Ralph, and to a startled and terrified ward.

"Aye…Wunt… *BLOODY JEWISH ALVER…*"

Chapter Four
Scots Wha' Hey!

'Oh my God,' muttered Fastovski in near-silent anguish. 'Is there no *beginning* to his talent?' The source of Fastovski's irritation which spawned the remark, was the dolt playing the penny whistle only some yards from where he was sitting and munching some toast and honey served by the lovely Pam, outside the café opposite the Heath. For the benefit of verity (Fastovski was somewhat of a stickler in this regard), the irritating minstrel was actually playing the piece reasonably accurately, but as he apparently knew no other, continued in a mournful monotone with the great Scots lament "Amazing Grace" in maddening... unremitting... repetition. Not that Fastovski was particularly averse to repetitiveness, indeed he somewhat revelled in his own mastery of the art. However, by way of amelioration there was nothing faintly humorous, or indeed ironic in the dreadful sounds emanating from the poisonous pipe which were annoying Fastovski...it was clear that the demented troubadour was not only murdering music, but more importantly (or so considered Fastovski) it was ruining his breakfast.

Only the previous morning, Fastovski had been driven near to madness whilst taking elevenses at the rather pretentious Café Salieri, just across the Heath, in Highgate;

by the same drone of anguish given by the same demented player-dope. On this occasion, the piper played almost within the tables set outside the café and seemingly without concern to the other diners two of whom to Fastovski's horror even placed money in his cap and exchanged pleasantries of some sort (a typical "champagne socialist" gesture). In order to maintain a hold both on his temper and sanity, Fastovski turned his thoughts to something which by comparison he considered idyllic, and from which he could console his hurt mind. Yes…the contemplation of the Naval Battle of Tsushima in 1904, between the Imperial Russian war fleet, and that of the Emperor of Japan, which he invariably employed on occasions such as these. Having eventually recovered his composure, Fastovski was again being subjected to the same ordeal as heretofore, and which was similarly destabilising his equanimity. A repetitive nightmare which seemed on a par with the great film on that subject, "Dead of Night" (Basil Cavalcanti 1946) starring Michael Redgrave and Mervyn Johns…which had maintained a haunting presence in the mind of the young Fastovski who had seen the film at the tender age of eight at the Kensington Cinema, deepest Liverpool. To be truthful the recalcitrant did attempt now and again to play "Mull of Kintyre" which was soon transmuting itself however back into "Amazing Grace"… He simply could not find his way out of the repetitive nightmare he (unconsciously perhaps) was trapped in, but in which Fastovski was now irrevocably drawn (and hung and quartered also) by the death-inducing sickly wheeze of wind.

Fastovski's mind was drawn back in time by this chaotic juxtaposition of melody and chord structures; into the remembrance of a small voice, uttering, 'Are-eh gissakick lah.' Denizens of Liverpool and Professors of Linguistics might recognise the plaintive whine emanating from the small tousle haired snotty nosed scuffed boots ragged trousered open gobbed urchin, pleading for a kick of the football that the equally young but well attired and presented Fastovski was kicking with some of his pals on the Triangle Field in Sefton Park.

'Orright then,' responded Fastovski's pal, "Chambo", and inviting the young scallywag to join them. Fastovski himself had he been inclined to proffer hospitality to the unsavoury intruder would have employed his rather "posh Liverpool" in which he expressed himself, rather than the parochially observed vernacular of his compatriots. As it was, the group was joined by a youth who named himself as Paul. He was rather slight in build with pronounced "saucer eyes", and was soon found vulnerable to the ferocious "Ray Lambert" death tackles of Fastovski in the "kick around" which followed. Good job it was only a "friendly".

Young Paul did have spirit though, and came back on some further occasions departing it may be said with an even greater variety of sprains and bruises.

Fastovski always gave credit where it was due however, and on the apotheosis some years later of the young scallywag into a greater divinity than Jesus Christ, did receive Fastovski's approbation entirely because it fed his sense of savage irony. It was Paul's friend John Lennon of course who made the claim on his own behalf and that of McCartney who by now had wisely given up playing football with Fastovski, but unwisely had taken up the guitar. Fastovski, however, was particularly vigilant in defence of both his own intellectual copyright and of others, and felt greatly offended by learning of the composition "Mull of Kintyre" (by "Macca" of course) which bore an amazin' resemblance to "Amazin' Grace"…and the remembrance of which was now being felt as a paean of torture to the now older Fastovski lost in his reminiscences in his favourite café on Hampstead Heath. He nevertheless garnered some comfort from the fact that at least (according to his knowledge) Macca had not *yet* claimed greater divinity than Ray Lambert (see p 21) or even God forbid! The Zeus of the great Liverpool Gods of football…Billy Liddell. He wouldn't put it past him though…and Jesus was no doubt a much better footballer than the young McCartney although with some strange infatuation with hanging from the crossbar, which, in the fixture of Israel v Italy at Jerusalem Stadium led to his being sent off.

Historical note:- the original fixture was played in Israel and the decision went to Italy whose Roman signings were proving quite deadly. A return fixture was arranged and scheduled to be played also in Israel but was called off due to crowd violence, and the Italian team and huge army of supporters (or what was left of them) was obliged to depart in some haste. The Israeli football hooligans pursued them back to Italy where they created violent disturbances, and everywhere else in the Roman Empire, before being placed under arrest; this particular fixture lasting some three years…with the referees in particular having a very hard time. Some of the Judean skinheads were in fact given bookings at the

73

"Colosseum" which at the time enjoyed a reputation somewhat similar to that of the "Pavilion" in Liverpool, or the Glasgow Empire. The decider referred to above was played some years later, and was notorious for the fact that whilst the Captain of the Israeli national team was fooling about in goal, he kept taunting the crowd, and asking them why their Manager had deserted them and apparently mocking the rest of his team for a poor performance, saying, 'They know not what they do!' The officials became increasingly vexed by his antics, showed him the red card, prised him off the cross bar (much to the annoyance of his mother) and locked him in the dressing room for three days, until he was eventually spirited away by his teammates. Harrumph! Certainly not in the same league as Ray Lambert, but considerably better however than Paul McCartney, who God help us; seemingly cannot be prised away from his guitar.

The strange thing about the whole episode was that the fifer-criminal seemed in appearance to be a world away from the emotional genesis and morbid sentimentality that any normal Scotsman would entertain for the song.

Indeed, whilst Fastovski felt deep sympathy for the heroic Highland uprisings of 1715 and 1745; (he thoroughly enjoyed abortive revolutions, uprisings and heroic failure…and was particularly attracted to all things Polish as a result)…he felt in his bones that the song may have been better received in The Shetlands, Faroes, Fair Isle or Rockall even, rather than in Hampstead where "Kumbaya" and other "songs" of "Brotherhood" seem more appropriate. It would certainly not have been appreciated in the Dagger Bank or German Bight, where the German lineage of "Bonnie Prince Charlie" would have been as recognisable as that of the present "Charlie" residing in degenerate opulence at Buck House, Balmoral, Windsor…and everywhere else in this disunited Kingdom where the demented self-regarding layabout draws his limitless benefit payments. Indeed, the previous "Bonny Prince Charlie" was in fact no more a Scotsman than the pie-eyed piper of Hampstead, who in appearance more likely resembled a Somali, Watutsi, or Masai from the Continent of Africa, than a piper in the "Black Watch" which possibly he thought he might in fact be. He seemed just a shade under seven foot tall, and unlike the "Charlie of the Isles" with his bucolic red face; or the self-regarding and pitiful "Charlie of Wails" with his sickly green Kermit like visage, the piper was unmistakably…err… Black.

At this juncture of his cerebral soliloquising, Fastovski felt it prudent to make it appear that he was studying the pages of "The Independent" which the previous table occupant had left behind and in the belief that it might deflect the possibility of attracting any accusation of non-Politically Correct thinking or "Racism" from any passing members of the Hampsted PC Thought Police; such as Glenda Jackson. The great Glenda (like Fastovski) was of Liverpudlian lineage where no doubt she was referred to as "Jacko" before the days that she had achieved (together with the equally loathsome Cherie Blair) her own divine apotheosis as a mixture of Mary Mother of God and the Mad Medusa. What is it about Liverpool? Perhaps the saddest irony of all was that the prescient fears articulated by George Orwell in his futuristic description of a Fascist England with its murder of individuality and dissent and omnipotent "Thought Police"…should receive its manifestation by those such as "Jacobin Jacko" who represented that very ward in which Orwell himself resided in South Hampstead and around the corner from Fastovski.

Fastovski actually did relish a good tune on the whistle and particularly admired Wee Willie McHastie, who played reeds for "The Temperance Seven"…which together with "Spike Jones and his City Slickers" and "Sid Millward and his Nitwits" he held in increasing esteem as the years flew by. Especially so in the case of the great Spike with his superb musicianship and manic lunacy. It did occur to Fastovski that if the fifing recalcitrant was passionately convinced (despite his appearance) of his own Scottish lineage; then likewise, McHastie (despite his "bull in the mooth" West Glasgow demeanour of pugnacity and all-too-obvious Pictish- Caucasian antecedents) might well consider himself a Watutsi, or Kikuyu for all we know. Fastovski resolved to test the theory the very next time he bumped into him at the 100 Club in Oxford Street. In the distorted psychosis of "World Music" and "Multicuturalism" which to Fastovski were two further manifestations of the suppression of individuality; it would seem quite appropriate that the lunatic Idi Amin would declare himself "King of Scotland" (as he did), and possibly employ a band of Scottish kilted Ugandan bandsmen rendering the Kampala version of "Amazin' Grace" where no doubt the subject of the present narrative received the entire sum of his musical education. Indeed, the somewhat surrogate "Scotsman" neither disported a set of Highland Bagpipes (Thank God/Lennon/McCartney) nor possessed an authentic and deep seated Scottish lineage complete with unmistakable Scottish surname such as say, Trevor McDonald, Sol Campbell or Moira Stuart…not forgetting Baroness

Scotland, leader of the House of Lords and look-alike of the fearsome Grace Jones... Now there's an Amazin' Grace if ever there was one.

Pursuing this line of thought where all individuality and difference is eliminated; it would follow logically that the Coronation of Wee Willy McHastie as Emperor of Uganda might already be in the planning stage. Indeed the recent enthronement of that Ugandan prime idiot John Sentamu ('e am nuts) as Archbishop of York...a ludicrous fool dressed in a frock, now busily converting (with the support of the Pathetic Prince of Wails and the WHITE Idiot -savant Archbishop of Canterbury...aka Druid Williams) of the Church of England into the Church of Islam...would seem to offer the politically correct quid pro quo with Wee Willie as "Da noo Empra" as King Idi of Scotland might have described it. Perhaps Emperor McHastie might then give his bandsmen leave to try out some new numbers...anything other however than "O Flower of Scotland" the new "Scottish National Anthem" which is without doubt the very worst piece of music ever written...ever. McCartney himself couldn't make it worse, but no doubt he'll try.

Fastovski ordered more tea, raised the steaming brew to his lips and contented himself that whatever the truth of all of this; he could console himself that in all probability it would be revealed in "The Independent" as some Zionist conspiracy by World Jewry, and that the Piper would be identified as an agent of Mossad.

Addendum

For purposes of verity, it should be stressed that Fastovski wrote the piece under the distinct impression that he had played football with Paul McCartney as described. He wishes to confirm however that it is solely a piece of artistic license, which nevertheless most certainly would have happened if the game had taken place. Everything else is true, and without any fabrication ***whatsoever.***

Leon Schmitt, a young Jewish cavalry officer in the Red Army had swaggeringly berated Josef Stalin on the steps of the Smolny Institute in the time-honoured manner of this elite fraternity. However, Stalin had now been confirmed as the General Secretary of the Communist Party and had instituted his reign of terror.

Schmitt's fellow officers urged him to apologise and upon which they agreed a form of words in writing. Brief and to the point... Cavalry fashion.

Comrade Koba

I was wrong; I was a fool; I should apologise.

Comrade Captain Leon Schmitt
1st Budenny Cavalry

Drinking some Vodka with his mates at a Tavern later on that evening, Schmitt confided that the message should be construed as, 'I was a *fool*? I was *wrong*? *I* should *apologise?*'

**Elimelech (Zeideh Feldman)
RAF 1939**

**Israel (Issy) Feldman, Home
Guard 1939**

**Issy, Fastovski, Nechamka
(Bobba Feldman) Rev 'Willy'
Wolfson 1965**

**Elimelech (Zeideh Feldman)
1953 'Are you looking at
me…eh?'**

Chapter Five
Whatever Happened to Terry Tan?

Fastovski was in very good mood that morning. The weather was cold but calm as to his taste, the sun was gently shining, and he had enjoyed his perambulation over the Heath to Highgate and intending to recuperate at the pretentious Café "Salieri" which was very popular amongst local denizens. He was delighted to discover that two doors away a little and very elegant café with few tables inside and two tables outside had opened but recently.

Fastovski considered that if any café maintained an atmosphere of pretentiousness, then it should at least provide something better than the ubiquitous aluminium tables and chairs which the "Salieri" considered good enough but which Fastovski in the exercise of his own defined pretentiousness (when it suited him), emphatically did not. The café next door provided comfortable chairs and tables of high quality and elegance in a vein of pertinent understatement and in this minimalist environment an atmosphere of calm and warmth pervaded. Thank goodness they didn't call it Café Stockhausen…

Apart from a Chinese gentleman of about the same age as Fastovski there were as yet no other clientele, but whilst drinking a very good Assam and nibbling on a crusty tasty croissant Fastovski's mind for some reason was drawn to Terry Tan and an episode long ago. Fastovski's creative and imaginative processes were (in the main) activated like this by food (but not drink), and especially so in the environment of a good café (but never in a restaurant). Whilst café society would stimulate the thought processes which fashioned his composition of Concerto and Big Band Jazz (and Operetta, in which he exercised his passion for whimsy) he found that such inspiration could sometimes also derive from the clearly non-thought processes of amour…quite normal of course. Certainly his Big Band Number "Soho in the Snow" was inspired by his lovely companion immediately after a session at "Ronnie Scotts", when at 3am, the snow was falling in Frith Street, the neon looked exactly like an American film noir of the 1940s and which they both regarded evocatively whilst sitting well wrapped up outside the "Bar Italia" where they recuperated on strong espresso whilst the snow fell evenly on them.

Fastovski smiled to himself and noticing that the Chinese gentleman was preparing to depart recalled another location which in every regard and in the passage of time he could regard as different in every conceivable regard from the Bar Italia. The "Slaughterhouse" they called it. Not a nice name, but nevertheless an apt description of the dark forbidding Gothic building in Hope Place nestling in the shadow of the looming presence of the great Anglican Cathedral. More correctly it was named "The Liverpool Hebrew Schools" (sic), and generally referred to as "The Jewish School". It had built up an unsavoury reputation (since its founding in 1840) for casual violence amongst the pupils, both boys and girls, referred to in those days as "scholars" and had attracted the most sadistic teachers imaginable who relished, participated, and seemingly encouraged a regime of terror. Certainly not all the Jewish kids in Liverpool attended this dreadful place, and certainly not all the teachers were sadistic. Those who were not, simply stood aside.

Pleasant Street School nearby was well run, orderly and tolerant and numbered about one third Jewish pupils who integrated perfectly and were very well treated. Indeed, Fastovski's mother and uncles had been alumni, and seemed as a consequence and in common with fellow pupils to exhibit greater balance, better behaviour and more dignified demeanour than the hooligans turned out by the Jewish School. Rathbone School had a smaller component of Jewish kids who again were treated well without any problems "in the playground". It was clear that the only place in the whole of Liverpool where a Jewish kid would be endangered was the Jewish School. Probably that's why Fastovski's parents insisted that he enrol. His father Issy had actually spent some two years there after his escape from Russia in 1922 and was beaten black and blue by staff and pupils alike. He would no doubt have been safer back in Odessa, where the Cossacks were no doubt better mannered.

Unusually for a Jewish school, it was run on secular lines without any requirement for the boys to cover their heads as the Jewish Schools in London and elsewhere did (and still do). Undoubtedly, Jewish Schools generally have a fine educational record and vie with the best, and in this regard the Liverpool Hebrew School produced its fair share of academics, professionals, entertainers, idiots, psychopaths and criminals. However, and because of their dominant religious ethos the other Jewish Schools elsewhere in the UK tend to breed a form of social insularity, which certainly did not apply to the kids at the "Slaughterhouse" who were anything but insular, and felt at ease both with themselves as Jews and with everybody else who were'nt. Liverpool is still like that, but London manifestly is not. The handful of religious kids in the Liverpool establishment sported the little skull cap or "Yamulka" and took the customary religious services. "Hebrew" however was on the curriculum, but secondary to the academic subjects. The "raison d'etre" of this institution was essentially in the turning out of Englishmen, hence its secular nature. Perhaps in so doing it consciously or otherwise endeavoured to emulate the nastier English Public Schools reputation for brutality. Who knows? The only teachers (with one or two exceptions) who were respected and liked by the kids were the few non-Jewish Staff. God knows what they were doing there…anyway they didn't last long. The tall gangly blond-haired Mr Jacobsen (of Viking ancestry) had been a soldier in Palestine, was very phsilo-semitic…was a marvellous teacher…and left after about one year or so.

No doubt the violence of the Irgun Zvei Leumi in Palestine had not afforded him sufficient battle-hardening to take on the battle conditions abounding in the dark recesses of the frightful establishment in Hope Place…or as it was referred to by the more perceptive and intelligent scholars; "The Place without Hope". Strangely, the school attracted a handful of non-Jewish kids from around the area who suffered the same terror as their Jewish classmates and in addition were obliged to endure being bashed up by them on occasion. A local tough of the name of "Crannie" certainly had a bad time and should not have been there…there were a few others too including the frightening hard case Lewis Cohen (Jewish father), and the well-loved gentle smiling Georgie Jones who sailed through without a scar physical or mental. Tribalism, that's all.

Jewish kids in places such as Smithdown Road and Lidderdale and elsewhere throughout Liverpool were subjected to similar treatment, and learned to "Stand their ground". All good building blocks naturally, for good Englishmen. Yes, the Christian kids were given the opportunity to spill their claret in a Jewish playground as well as any attendee of Eton, Marlborough or Rugby, or for that matter Jewish kids in Odessa or Oldham. All that is except for Terry Tan whose genesis was somewhat different…

The Liverpool Chinese Community is recognised as the oldest and largest in Europe and dating from about 1750. Sailors and merchants, they originated mainly from Shanghai and Hong Kong and brought the women later. They settled in the vicinity of Seel Street which at that time was adjacent to the Jewish Community who built their first Synagogue in that very street. The Jewish Community has both shrunk and moved on since those days whilst the Chinese Community has basically remained in the same area. As a child Fastovski used to frequent the restaurants in the area with his parents and unlike the heavily Europeanised variety of Chinese Restaurant which abound both in Liverpool (sadly) and throughout the rest of the UK, these were the real thing. The menus were either in Chinese or didn't exist, and the clientele was a heady mixture, with a very high proportion of Jews slurping their bowls of noodles sometimes louder than their fellow Chinese diners and shouting loudly across the room. The Christian diners ate very fastidiously (as they did in those days) and as if they were dining on corned beef and lettuce (with a little tomato and diced beetroot and thin white bread and butter) for supper or high tea at home in their own parlours whilst endeavouring not to display under any circumstances any sense of enjoyment whatsoever and most certainly without speaking which would have been bad manners and ensuring most determinedly both that their mouths remained closed and that their jaws did not move. The jocular Jews jaws moved with unrestrained abandon, (as did those of the Chinese). Both tribes loved their food and didn't mind showing this in the least, and without any restriction whatsoever on mouth/jaw mobility. It may well be for this reason that the Tans sent Terry to the Jewish School which was only five minutes slurp from "Kwok Fongs" eating house, the oldest and best establishment, and on whose steps some years later, Fastovski's mother (who in most regards a very sensible woman), was engaged in conversation for some minutes with a young man who she mistook for the young Fastovski. Luckily, his father was on hand to advise her that the young gentlemen was *NOT* her son but was in fact a young man called Karl who bore an uncanny resemblance to her own offspring. Karl and Fastovski were very pally but not close friends and as a consequence were rarely seen in each other's company. On more than one occasion, each was mistaken for the other and sometimes in circumstances of almost Shakespearean comedy (the incident at Kwok Fongs would attest to this)…not that Fastovski's mother had been unaware of the uncanny resemblance between the two. Anyway, as was being previously alluded to, the Tans no doubt considered the Jewish School would turn their young son into a proper Englishman…and why not indeed…and that presumably is why he had been named in the English fashion. In those days, the Chinese whilst well liked were considered somewhat comical, and the butt of jokes relating to "slitty eyes" (ref various pronouncements by the Duke of Edinburgh); Chinese Laundries ("No tickee no washee") Mr Wu (as sung by George Formby) chopsticks, pigtails, and so on. Terry however was never ever to endure these indignities in "The Slaughterhouse". Despite the fact that he spoke not a word of English everybody took him under his (or her) wing, cossetted him, and helped him with sincere deep affection and friendship. Language of course doesn't matter to kids who are perfectly capable of communicating without it, and in the course of his stay in the school of some short duration became reasonably proficient in Scouse, and quite well versed in Yiddish including some colourful expletives; which no doubt in the fullness of time have now entered the Liverpool Cantonese lexicon. Probably in the slightly more genteel academies of Pleasant Street and Rathbone, he might have been made into mincemeat, if not dim sum.

Violence in this august establishment was not restricted to the playground. Soon after Fastovski's joining the school, his teacher put her head in the gas oven and committed suicide. It was an open secret apparently that she had carried on a long-standing affair with the headmaster, and it may have been something to do with that. In addition, the unfortunate lady was bullied openly by another lady member of staff, Miss Sarapski; where the two shared the same classroom with different groups concurrently (in educational terms the "Lancastrian system" which was introduced into the English educational system circa 1840) and as a consequence she drew a great deal of sympathy from the "scholars" Both of these ladies had never married. The headmaster "retired", to be succeeded by a most benign and seemingly affable gentleman which smarmy façade however concealed a venal malignancy of which Fastovski was to suffer consequences later, and prior to his own escape "over the wire" to High School. The scoundrel posing as "Headmaster" went on to achieve eminence in educational and "consultative" circles in the London Jewish Community. A fitting punishment no doubt. Sadly, the new teacher Miss Best, was similarly bullied by the fearful Sarapski, and would pop round to see young Fastovski whenever he was bedridden with bronchitis which seemed to continue with increasing frequency until treatment from Professor Sir Henry Cohen controlled it with a regimen of steroids, some three years later. Both Tilly and Fastovski were aware of her sad life and of her deep loneliness and a cup of tea and biscuit was always supplied to her, and she would sit at Fastovski's bedside talking of this and that. She would eat Fastovsk's biscuits however. At around the same time (when Fastovski had turned five) Issy took him to

Greenbank Synagogue to join the Cheder (religious classes, in preparation for the Barmitzvah Ceremony at age thirteen…where Hebrew and Jewish ethics and philosophy would be studied) Issy asked his son if he felt nervous. Fastovski responded that he felt OK and jokingly remarked that it would be fine provided that it was anybody but Miss Sarapski. Issy laughed, and on entering the Hall found Her great Herself sitting there behind the desk with eyes of demonic red, and with a terrifying rictus of a smile, Fastovski froze.

Indeed, Fastovski's baptism into violence at the school occurred within a week or two of his joining and well before he had a chance of settling in properly.

Adjacent to the School in Hope Place was a house or two at which certain local ladies used to entertain Polish airmen. The Yanks in their posh "Atlantic House" in Hardman Street on the other side of the School frequented more "classy" establishments elsewhere. The "Scholars" relations with the yanks were excellent and the kids would (on asking) usually find themselves in possession of a stick or two of chewing gum. The big smiling Black Yanks were especially kind and popular with the Jewish kids. Relations with the Poles were. cordial in the extreme and were personified mainly by verbal insults on either side. Quite normal. However, it was the custom of some of the local Christian kids either to attack the Jewish lads individually or on occasion to join forces and commit to a full-scale attack on the School itself, and in which instance the "scholars" would come out somewhat in a "levee en masse" to do battle; provided of course that the numbers seemed not too disproportionate. If considerably outnumbered, however, it was considered prudent to stay inside the playground where both sides in gestures of friendship and cordiality lobbed milk bottles (both empty and unemptied) and bricks over the wall. On one memorable occasion, whilst kicking a tennis ball with some of his classmates there was a sudden rush to the School Gate, into which the young scholar in his newly pressed uniform was drawn; only to find a mass of scruffy kids standing at the top of Hope Place hurling stones and insults on the Jewish Lads who were gathering forces at the bottom of the Hill about 50 yards distant. The assailants eventually charged down screaming like Highlanders and chucking stones, but were received very much like Englishmen at Culloden, and sent packing back up the Hill, pursued by the "scholars" only to be repulsed, as was Williams Cavalry by Harold's "Hus Carls" at Hastings in similar topographical/tactical circumstance. This time, the Jewish lads were overwhelmed and pushed back towards the School Gate with the younger boys being pulled back in by the girls. Fastovski, however, was outflanked and found himself all alone and standing on some ancient iron grating by the wall whilst fighting raged all around him, and unable to reach the gate whilst the girls were holding out their hands and increasingly anxious for him.

Young Fastovski lived in one of the "Dales" down Smithdown Road, and numbered amongst his neighbours, the Lansky's, two roads away. A jolly, smiling family of six and all remarkably tough (both boys and girls), with Morris the toughest of the lot. Like the Fastovski's they too had hailed from Elizavetgrad and knew each other's family very well. Morris was standing near to Fastovski and hitting out in all directions with the blood lust of a

Viking…or more likely of a Lansky. Fastovski sensed rescue and shouted to Morris to help him to the gate. Unfortunately by this time, Lansky was in something akin to a personal bar room brawl in a "Western" and was hitting out indiscriminately, and somehow or other did not seem to heed the polite request from the endangered little boy, but responded by smashing his heavy fist into Fastovski's face…splattering his nose and drenching his rough grey viyella shirt and new uniform and the grime ridden grating on which he stood, with his blood. Some girls very bravely and at great risk to themselves opened the gate and grabbed Fastovski back inside where he was by now somewhat shocked, and in need of an urgent staunch. The young casualty was borne down the cold stone stairs of the forbidding building by three of the girls, with two holding a leg each and the third one standing behind him supporting his head (and nose) and transporting him into the dining room/dressing station in the bunker under the dreadful school. The nose responded quite quickly to a firmly applied tea towel, with the lovely Nancy (and head girl…no less) holding his hand whilst sitting beside him on the bench. After a little while, Nancy looked at him and with (what he thought, with some regret) told him gently that she had better go back upstairs, kissed him on the cheek and pressed into his hand a piece of carrot and turnip from the dining room, which constituted "dessert" for school dinners in wartime Liverpool.

The violence continued in one form or another until well after VE.DAY, and having abated on 1945 recontinued during the dreadful anti-Jewish riots in

Liverpool over three days during the August bank holiday of 1947, including one quite startling occasion when a passing coal lorry stopped outside the school during a quite large melee, and locating itself behind the Jewish lads, the driver and mate proceeded to hurl huge chunks of coal at them, seriously outflanking them and putting them in acute danger. However, nobody was hurt too badly as the coalmen seemed to perform their artillery in a rather perfunctory manner whilst being berated for "foul play" and such-like terminology; to which they seemed to respond good naturedly by eventually ceasing this dangerous activity. Unusually, the new Headmaster appeared, and with his whistle ushered the kids back in. Nobody could remember any of the staff previously coming to their assistance; as no doubt they saved their energies for the further brutalisation of their charges on their return from the Battlefield. Fastovski in particular had seemingly insoluble problems with Bender, the Senior Hebrew Teacher; an elderly, dirty fingernailed creature with various other disgusting habits of an unhygienic nature. Fastovski would not work in this class and was continually being sent down to the class run by the arch-sadist Kauffmann who had the bearing, manner, and appearance of the stereotypical SS Officer (complete with blond hair and blue eyes, and much like Dinsdale Landen the film actor (also Jewish) who specialised in sadistic SS Officer roles…perhaps he had been a pupil somewhere of Kauffmann). The demonic Hebrew teacher would elevate his unfortunate victims by twisting their cheek almost off their face whilst virtually hanging them at tip toe, and all performed with the slow sadistic smile of the true

SS…perhaps he was actually trained by the Gestapo. Stranger things have happened. Adolf Eichmann, a fluent Hebrew speaker had lived before the war in Israel ("Palestine" – for readers of the "Independent". "The Guardian" and listeners to the "BBC", and not wishing to exclude all those left/liberal/fascist apologists for suicide bombing in Israel (not "Palestine" this time!) such as Cherie Blair, Glenda Jackson, George Galloway, and Ken Livingstone, and their respective martyr-seeking cohorts.) Incidentally when George Orwell had been asked in 1943 as to whether he modelled his English fascist State in his book "1984" on Hitler's Germany or Stalin's Russia he advised the enquirer that it was modelled entirely on the BBC, and the enemy "Goldstein" in that terrifying book has now become "Sharon" or "Begin" or "Golda Meir" (the lady who had the temerity to order the hunting down of the murderers of the Israeli Athletes at Munich); or indeed of anybody else anywhere who supports the Jewish State. This device of hatred against "The Zionist" "the other", "the rootless Jew" (and now "America" which is a mutated code-name for "Jewish Influence") conceals a malodorous surrender of everything appertaining to English tolerance and decency and replaces it with the oozing fascist miasma of political correctness and "multiculturism" which is destroying the very fabric of our society with increasing and effective rapidity. Dear me; mere words just do not explain.

For some reason Kauffmann actually seemed to like Fastovski as much as Bender hated him, with the result being his constant perambulation between the two classes where he alternatively came top and bottom. "Top of the Bottom, and Bottom of the Top" as he would relate the story. Nevertheless, Fastovski managed somehow to win the prize for the year in Hebrew, but for reasons of limited seating (so they said!) was excluded from the prize day ceremony at the prestigious Picton Hall despite the ineffectual protest of his parents. Perhaps, the school Gauleiters feared that Fastovski might institute an uprising or riot or whatever similar. Nevertheless, it was some consolation for the young somewhat cerebral scallywag to have received a rather good monetary reward as his prize; which he cashed in (as required) at the Jewish Board of Guardians when its Chief Officer, the good Manny Felton expressed his disgust at what had happened. There were further instances where certain favoured "scholars" (generally the son/daughters of influential/wealthy members of the community) received noticeably preferential treatment including unmerited prizes to the disadvantage of some others and notably of Fastovski. One grossly improper decision of the headmaster was again contested by Fastovski's parents but to no avail, as the Board of Governors backed the headmaster. Fastovski was the school star at music, and quite gifted at the piano where he would regularly perform at school concerts. He was however not denied any prize in this subject, presumably because one was not awarded.

Postscript

Fastovski and his pal Mass (who resembled the actor Richard Todd with his limpid blue twinkling eyes: a handsome kid) had been given places after the eleven-plus at a High School in "Judenrein" North Liverpool where they approached the certainty of being very much in the minority "amongst the Christians" without any real concern, but recognising that nevertheless they should be on their guard. Assigned to the same class, true enough they were the only Jewish kids present. The register was called out by Miss McCann a gorgeous red head and afterwards took a note firstly of Catholics (very much in the majority…*NORTH* Liverpool) and then Protestants (a sizeable minority…there had after all been a Reformation, even in Liverpool apparently)…and then closed the register. Fastovski and Mass quickly conferred as to whether they should "stay schtum" but decided that it would be better to own up at the beginning rather than be found out later. In unison they put up their hands and advised Miss McCann that they were both Jewish. Immediately forty assorted Christians kids swivelled around as one to stare at the two yids in astonished disbelief, whilst the teacher effected an air of too-obvious insouciance, and so registered the two eleven-year-old killers of Christ. For the remainder of the lesson, the two were continually regarded by their fellow classmates who stared at them with intense curiosity as if possibly they were observing some mythical beast (or two). When the bell rang, the two pals walked out not too quickly and took care to keep close together to find themselves being encircled slowly by six of the boys whilst the two Jewish lads shifted their position gently in order to stand nearly back-to-back…just like John Wayne and Ward Bond anticipating an attack from Red Indians (Many films available from British Film Institute, on the subject.) True enough the circle slowly closed, and the natives opened up some initial verbal reconnaissance, the response to which might determine the fate of the two encircled Jewish lads. Jones *(moving closer to Fastovski whilst looking closely at him)* ...

'What's it like being a Jew?'

Fastovski *(looking Jones in the eye and taking care not to blink)* ... 'Great!'

Norton *(similarly staring at Mass, as if trying to find something)* ...

'My dad says all Jews have horns growing out their head.'

Mass 'We haven't.'
(spoken as if they should know, and delivered with the right degree of scorn)

(*pregnant pause...and 'stand off'*)

Kilgallon 'You're right...you 'aven't.'

This seemed to satisfy the interlocutors, and immediately Patrick Kilgallon, and the other boys invited the two valiant yids to play a game of "footie" with a tennis ball in the school playground, and to which they assented.

Undoubtedly their intensive training in emotional and physical violence at the "Slaughterhouse" did after all prove to be of some tangible benefit, and Fastovski in this instance quite wisely eased up a little on his Ray Lambert death tackles...just to be on the safe side.

Liverpool Education Committee.

School.. Department............................

Report........................... Term......................... 194..

Standard.. 5

Roll............

Name of Scholar... *Wallace Fields* Place............

Attendance... 62/89 Conduct... *Good*

Scripture *fairly good*	Arithmetic : *V. Good*
	Science ....
English :	Drawing ...... *V. Good*
Reading... *V. Good*	Physical Exercises ....
Writing... *V. Good*	Handwork ....
Spelling... *V. Good*	Other Subjects................
Composition... *V. Good*	
History... *V. Good*	
Geography ... *V. Good*	

Remarks... *Wallace works very well. He has made very good progress.*

(Signed)... *D. Raliff* .... Class Teacher.

E S Comlay .... Head Teacher.

Mr Bender
(Hebrew teacher, doppelganger of Boris Karloff
and avowed enemy of Fastovski)
accords the young man a 'fairly good' for
winning the Hebrew prize

Issy at ten with sister Eva and mother Nechamka, Elizavetgrad 1922

With parents, Tilly, Issy 1939

With Issy and Tilly, Blackpool 1948

Chapter Six
Moss Bros

"Fatso slung a low left hook and connected to the midriff of his taller and leaner opponent; evincing a gasping breath of pain and doubling him up from the vicious punch. He followed up quickly, bringing his two interlinked fists into his opponent's chin, rocking back his head and splattering his teeth with froth and blood from the devastating blow…"

Fastovski chuckled to himself as something drew him back to this opening line from a Hank Janson detective novel which he had read in his early teens. The "Hank Janson" books were written in the style of Film Noir 1940s New York and were peopled by "Tough Guys" "Broads" and "Dames"; people who were distinctly of more interest than the "touchy feely" Liberal Fascists with their sickening political correctness that now seemed to people the world of 2006.

They certainly dressed better, spoke better, and compared to the slovenly genus that now represented humanity; had style. People who saw things as they really were and called a spade a "Sam Spade". Language meant language and had not yet commenced its degenerate decline into the bland inoffensive "inclusive" jargon that now passed for verbal intercourse...

Jeez! Talkin' a intercourse buddy, can you imagine a cool, cigarette smoking Humphrey Bogart requesting a consensual document signature from a languid Ingrid Bergman? (Probably witnessed no doubt by Inspector Renault, for the consideration of a bottle or two of Krug.)

No, it wasn't the thought of the above scenario that made Fastovski chuckle into his toast and honey served "pain brule" just the way he liked it and by the lovely Pam who had greeted him with one of her special slow smiles which he did find very appealing. It was the memory of his new dinner jacket and the name "Moss Bros" on the label which he had adorned a few days previously for a piano recital which he had given at Hampstead Town Hall, which triggered the thought process of another who had similarly engaged in (seemingly perpetual) violence with his taller and leaner sparring partner.

However, in this particular case, the combatants were in fact brothers...of the name of MOSS... Ronnie (the fat one) was a year older than Laurie (the tall lean one) and at home there were two or more sisters; one of whom went to the High School that Fastovski attended, and brought with her the "Moss demeanour" which guaranteed safety from attack. The Moss Bros shared a waxy, pallid visage with a rather sickly smile and dead eyes; offset by fiery red hair. Outside of their tempestuous relationship with each other they seemed to rub along quite well generally with the other boys in Fastovski's extended circle of acquaintances, and any residual anger and spleen would seem (in the main) to be vented against their own eye popping dead eyed waxen visaged sibling. They actually hailed from London's East End and so possessed Cockney accents which however never seemed to be turned against them by the waggish Liverpool boys. Not surprising really. Invariably at events in which they participated they would end up fighting, especially so in football and in cricket too where on one occasion they set about each other with stumps.

Ronnie played centre forward in the Haroldean 2nd Team in which Fastovski at that time was captain, and indeed it was clear that Fastovski whilst rarely a dirty player did commit himself to the death tackle tactics of Ray Lambert to such effect that he earned Ronnie's grudging respect and compliance on the field of play; except for one very famous and indeed notorious occasion.

Violent conduct was no stranger to the Liverpool Jewish Community, and certainly on the football pitch it was by no means limited to the Moss Bros. Perhaps, the greatest victim/practitioner of the "red mist" was the famed Haroldean first team goalkeeper, the wonderfully appelled Edwin Marshall Klein. Whilst certainly not a Prussian, perhaps Eddie's temperament was fashioned to some extent at least by a name which could well have graced the same invitation list as that of Marshall's Hindenburg, Ludendorf, von Schlieffen, von Moltke etzetera, etzetera, etzetera. All good Prussians certainly, but no doubt far less violent in instinct than Marshall Klein, and certainly far more disciplined. Research has failed to uncover any instance whatsoever of any of the aforementioned gentlemen being awarded the red card at such social occasions as Tannenberg, Passchendale, or the Somme. On Marshal

Kleins chosen field of battle however, the Northern Jewish Soccer League; there was a distinct mathematical correlation between his "red mist" and "red card". Nevertheless, whilst Marshal Klein did not have the honour of directing (and completing) the battle of Tannenberg as had Marshal Ludendorf; Ludendorf had in return been denied any opportunity to do battle in the Nothem Jewish Soccer League (as incidentally had a gentleman bearing the name of his illustrious colleague Hindenburg, but more of that later)… Nevertheless, there did exist a strange quid pro quo between the two warriors, in that whilst Marshal Klein bore a distinct physical resemblance to Richard Wagner, Ludendorf spoke Yiddish (but not with a Liverpool accent), and addressed his Polish-Jewish troops in that lingo during a parade in Warsaw. Wagner however probably never sang "Rock Island Line" with the same manic intensity as did Marshall Klein…und danke Gott for that.

Eddie was a great pal of Fastovski's with a similar sense of the absurd and an exhibitionist streak which had led them both into the world of entertainment. Eddie had done quite a lot of stand-up comedy, and compering; under the name of "Mister Mirth". When Fastovski formed his "West Coast Skiffle Group" in 1956 Eddie was on third guitar, with Fastovski second guitar/banjo and vocal harmony to "Enna", lead singer and first guitar and later to earn fame as the victim of the bacon sandwich episode in Polly's Milk Bar after returning from National Service in Malaya (p 4). The tall wall-eyed and bespectacled Jackie Cohen from Southport was on double bass with Ray "Cake" Wasserman on washboard. Later the band was augmented by the brilliantly talented brother and sister Malcolm and Avril

Eleen on "Django" style acoustic guitar and mandolin, respectively. All the boys in the band were in love with Avril, but nevertheless, paid their attention to other girls. Many years later, Avril appeared in the audience at one of Fastovski's orchestral concerts at the Royal Festival Hall, and she was as beautiful and young as ever. The Skiffle Group was indeed very good; was booked at top venues around Merseyside and Manchester and indeed played on a number of occasions at the famed "Cavern" where after a hectic and exciting year the band broke up through the competing demands of University and National Service.

Eddie's football career as goalkeeper for the Haroldeans first team produced a total of 29 "sendings off" for various infringements, mostly involving punching the head of an opponent if beaten in the air. On the ground Eddie was an effective and very courageous goalkeeper, but his lack of height (only 5' 6", a little unusual for a goalkeeper) forced Eddie to "mix it" with the taller and more powerfully built centre forwards. Eddie however was a gentlemen and would not resort to such hooligan behaviour as kicking or gouging, which however he probably employed to some extent whilst playing Rugby for Merchant Taylors; a fine Public School which he attended. Eddie in later years would claim that his reputation was such that he earned some sendings off even prior to the commencement of the game. His most notorious achievement was in knocking out the famed Tobias, centre forward "glamour boy" of Manchester Jewish Working Men, and avowed enemies of the Liverpool team, during a match played in Calderstones Park, Liverpool. That afternoon, the Manchester boys were giving the Liverpool lads a drubbing and Eddie was building up a dangerous brew of anger and frustration at the seemingly endless repetition of picking the ball up from the back of the net.

Halfway through the second half, Tobias was again speeding towards the Liverpool goal whilst wrong footing the entire defence. On this occasion, Eddie ran out to meet him, and without any pretence of playing the ball hit Tobias on the chin knocking him out cold and standing over his vanquished enemy and gloating openly as did Maxie Baer over Primo Carnero at Madison Square Garden.

There is always a moment in human affairs either of the social or political nature, when time seems to stand still, maybe for only a moment when thereafter things change with unforeseen consequences. Such had occurred no doubt before the opening salvo of the Russian Battleships against their Japanese enemy in the Straits of Tsushima in 1904, and the other was the response to the unprovoked "chinning" of the Great Tobias by Edwin Marshal Klein. Twenty two footballers stood suspended in momentary space and time; eleven of whom then began moving towards Eddie with increasing momentum prompting his back pedalling for a few seconds, and deciding that discretion, in this particular instance certainly being the better part of valour, turned on his heel and fled for his life across the park with the now rabid Manchester boys rapidly closing in on their intended prey…somewhat like a gang of slavering wolves chasing "Roadrunner" of the famous cartoons. It certainly seemed nemesis for Eddie, and reminiscent somehow of the denouement of the tank battle of Kursk in 1943 (when another Prussian had similarly "done a runner") when out of the blue a saloon car driven by the great Herr Doktor Klein, Eddie's father (and from whom he had inherited his ferocious temper) came hurtling diagonally across the park whilst speeding alongside the retreating Marshal, and into which he hurled himself through the open door. Rommel, or Guderian himself could not have executed a finer manoeuvre with his tanks. The match was abandoned.

Arnold "Enna" Endfield (the skinny kid from Anfield) had joined the Jewish School some three years after Fastovski, and they became close pals instantly. Enna in appearance was something akin to Jakie Finkelfeffer, skinny, with an engaging personality allied to a nervous energy, unsmiling with a somewhat sallow complexion, and with a mass of unruly black curly hair. Possessed of an excellent nasal "Country and Western" style voice he and Fastovski would spend time singing music from Schubert to sea shanties with Fastovski providing the role of harmony. It was this harmony both of music and friendship which led to Fastovski forming the West Coast Skiffle Group. At about this time, they were asked to form an acapella singing group by their youth club to enter a Merseyside competition, in which the judges were some of the distinguished music teachers and other local icons. They recruited a singer who possessed a "tenor profundo", whilst Enna would sing "silver tenor", and Fastovski with "alto". For some reason, they elected to sing "Davy Crockett" (Born on a mountain top in Tennessee, free'est layand in the layand of the free…) heavens know why, possibly something to do with Fastovski's anarchic streak, but more likely because Enna by this time was singing "good ol' boy" songs of the American South and effecting a sort of Scouse/Savannah slow drawl which he has retained to this very day. Regrettably, it was soon discovered that the tenor was not entirely suited to the exigencies of close harmony…and their attempt at old-fashioned "barbershop" was not exactly destined for success.

The tenor profundo belted it out and provided a good vehicle for the harmonies supplied by Enna and Fastovski. Regrettably, his pitch was clearly slipping almost imperceptibly. Whatever remedial measures attempted by Enna and Fastovski quickly came to grief, and rather than withdraw from the contest they elected to enter it representing the entire Jewish Youth of Merseyside in a festival of some standing, and in a state of some clear imperfection, but hoping for the best as it were. On the great day, the boys preceded by a number attempts by young lads from local youth clubs all performing "The Lincolnshire Poacher" on self-made miniature xylophones about one foot in length. Possibly had their own contribution been performed in its entirety and as indifferently as the other competitors then that might have been acceptable to the illustrious adjudicators. As it was, nervous sniggering broke out at some point from Enna when it was clear that the pitch was beginning to waver and made more painful by the foghorn bellowing of the lead singer…the song died out; with a barked reprimand from the chief invigilator to "start again". On this occasion, laughter emanated from both Enna and Fastovski simply on catching each other's eye…another false start. Fastovski took it up upon himself to apologise to the judges, pleaded for the opportunity for another try, which was granted and at which point he positioned the boys somewhat in the figure of an outlandish outward looking triangle in a desperate effort to avert catching each other's eye; a solution less dictated by logic perhaps than by Fastovski's over indulgence in military imagery. Nemesis. The ensuing racket of misplaced notes, bellowing, choking laughter and "the Enna snigger" prompted the angry red-faced interruption of the chief judge who was now in a state of unconcealed apoplectic red-faced rage. 'An absolute disgrace…you have brought shame on yourselves, discredit on your Youth Club …dishonour on your community.' (The boys bridled a little at the latter remark but held their tongues)…and were ordered off the stage. Obviously, the adjudicators had preferred lumpen endeavour, to inventive genius. The boys reported the events to their club leader who simply nodded, and the matter was never raised again. In the following year, the club received an invitation for the next open music festival, and this time, Fastovski accompanied a good crooner, somewhat in the style of Dickie Valentine in the popular song "Rags to Riches"… 'Oh I will go from rags to riches, if you will only say you care…' Roger, dressed in a good suit and wide "herring bone" tie sang superbly, whilst Fastovski who by this time was a fully seasoned piano accompanist on the Liverpool cabaret scene supported him as any professional would. The boys were conceded a "well done", but no prize. At least they stayed to the end and noticed that on this occasion the Lincolnshire Poacher had deigned to attend.

Fastovski had auditioned for the Greenbank Synagogue Choir, where they demanded choristers of good musical standard and facility with sight reading, and he was thereupon appointed as Alto. The problem however and there certainly was a problem was that the Choir Master was unaware (at that stage) of Fastovski's anarchic streak which could be set off by all manner of things, but especially by Rabbis. The consequence was that Fastovski was unable to conceal his amusement at the unfortunate Officiant and would (whilst not laughing at him) make surreal comments "under his breath" which would set off the rest of the choir who would struggle desperately to stifle their laughter whilst seemingly choking to death. This caused an immense problem for the Choirmaster who because of his distinct resemblance to the character in the "Flash Gordon" films which Fastovski used to see at the Clayton Square News Theatre with his Uncle Joe was referred to by Fastovski as "Ming The Merciless". Anarchy and chaos ensued as a result which at times was punctuated however by some fine singing, and of growing bemusement by the congregation. As the sole alto, Fastovski would be paid 7/6d per month, whilst the sopranos would earn five shillings. On pay day however Fastovski would be "docked" 2/6d for bad behaviour but was nevertheless retained in the choir by the admirable and exceedingly patient "Ming". When they both left the choir soon after, they would invariably sit together at Saturday morning services, making pejorative remarks about the new choirmaster.

Not that Fastovski had any antipathy to members of the sacred calling, but in general terms, he considered their lack of humour, intelligence, scholarship and breeding allied to an overindulgence in pomposity to be worthy of his selective and often unconcealed scorn. He nevertheless did reserve a particular antipathy for the questionable Lubavitch movement that years later whilst posing as "friends" had targeted his lovely, funny high-spirited daughter Rachel; whilst the family was undergoing a crisis and therefore vulnerable…their widely practiced modus operandi which brought distress and disunity to many families. Nevertheless, whilst in Liverpool, he did have an ally in the Chief Minister at the Greenbank Synagogue, who himself was well possessed of all the qualities so lacking in his contemporaries (or most of them at least). The Reverend "Willy" Wolfson was one of that select breed of "Mountain Jews" from Tredegar in South Wales, and in possession of a pronounced anarcho-Welsh streak. The most brilliant after dinner speaker and debater that Fastovski had ever heard, and something akin to a Jewish Aneurin Bevan (another hero of the young Fastovski) also from Tredegar.

Willy Wolfson "kept an eye" on the young scallywag in the choir and encouraged his music and expression of his personality. He helped Fastovski understand his deep seated but unorthodox Jewishness and endorsed his free thinking. Many years later, he was guest of honour at Fastovski's wedding in London's East End. Fastovski also formed a close friendship with the Saintly Reverend Gerald Schneider and also with Reverend Sidney Black who had in earlier years been chaplain to the Socialist Zionist movement "Habonim" (or in English, "The Boys") in which Fastovski forged his love for and life-long commitment to Israel and Zionism. Rev Black followed in the footsteps of the great Rabbi Kook who similarly in the early days of the Jewish pioneers reclaiming the marshes and swamps of the land destroyed by centuries of neglect; had celebrated their Jewishness through their efforts both to rebuild themselves and their homeland and through their dedication to the soil. Rev Schneider had tried very hard but without success to help save Fastovski's failing marriage, and was a man who lived on the same axis as Fastovski, "Willy" Wolfson and Sidney Black.

It was not only Fastovski who revelled in persecuting the Jewish Ministry. Two close friends of his; Harry "Slag heap" Davies (so named in ironic deference to his undeniable elegance and fastidiousness) and Ivan "the truly terrible" Goldberg, named as such for exploits which need another book…at the very least. Both members of the Haroldeans FC first eleven, Harry was at centre half and played very much in the vein of the classy and ill-fated Laurie Hughes the Liverpool player. Ivan played (nominally) at right half and with a thuggish smiling aggression and high stepping sod-churning industry which deterred all but the most foolhardy from approaching him (on or off the field).

Travelling back together from somewhere in the posh Liverpool district of Allerton from somewhere or other; they were sitting on the upstairs on the backseat of the open backed routemaster bus, and laughing gently at he mixed selection of humanity which were appearing at the top of the stairs…head, neck, shoulders; trunk; legs; in sequence which to the boys appeared increasingly surreal and very funny. The owner of the aforementioned appurtenances would then stop for an instant, regard the environment and then make a decision as to where to sit. Each successive passenger set the two boys laughing a little louder, to that point where it may well have caused offence, with some of the passengers looking back with varying degrees of amusement. There was a slight pause followed by the hesitant appearance of a black rabbinical Homburg, followed slowly by a pair of glasses, scrawny beard, of a black-clad slight rather owlish figure which they recognised as the Reverend Woolf with whom they were acquainted. On reaching the top of the stairs, Reverend Woolf gazed in a startled and helpless manner at the two brutes (he no doubt had a premonition); which was of course the very worst thing that he possibly could have done under the circumstances - and thereby in an instant earned the sobriquet of the "Sheep in woolf's clothing" from the exultant "Slag Heap". Much, much worse was to follow. The boys gave up any pretence at stifling their laughter and bellowed at him with uncontrolled body-splitting hysteria; in which some of the upper deck joined in; Jew and Christian alike. The poor Rabbi simply stood transfixed and unblinking in a state of shock; whilst being pointed at dramatically by "Ivan the truly Terrible" and greeted with a wolfs howl as "The Black Rab-yool"... The Black Rab-yool!!!" to which the poor unfortunate responded by opening and closing his mouth somewhat like a fish out of water; or more appropriately a Gefilte fish in onion stock (with a little lemon and horseradish on the side preferably) Matters only became worse when the miserable unfortunate took the only option available to him, and descended the stairs very slowly backwards, to conclude finally with his rabbinical hat which wavered slightly and which then followed the socially drowned unfortunate and very much in the manner of Buster Keaton in a possible similar scenario.

Denouement

The Haroldean's first eleven had been suffering a poor set of results, whilst the second eleven under the captaincy of Fastovski were proving a tight combination and winning most of their games. At some juncture in the season, neither team had a game lined up for some reason and it was decided that they should play each other. On the day, and during the dressing room briefing Fastovski had impressed upon the team the necessity to maintain discipline, and assured them that they could beat their rather "flash" and "arrogant" opponents. This necessary injection of appropriate hatred had commenced on the arrival of the two teams, which despite close friendships had just the correct degree of animosity, as one would expect. Fastovski took the added precaution of taking Ronnie Moss (centre forward) aside and received his assurances that he would avoid any conflict with his brother Laurie, his opponent at centre half in the opposing team. The first team included Marshall Klein, "Slag Heap", "Ivan the truly terrible", and other stalwarts. The second team included "Cake" Wassermann, Mike Hindenburg and "Farmer" Clayman as well as Ronnie Moss and Fastovski himself. Once underway, the second team took immediate control, and within ten minutes were awarded with a fine goal, which an angry Marshall Klein picked up from the back of the net. This set up the expected rush of blood to the first team which attacked powerfully but were well held by the strong and coordinated defence organised by Fastovski, and in which "Cake" and "Farmer" particularly were proving very strong and effective. Niggles set in as the somewhat perturbed first eleven found themselves being outwitted now seemingly at every turn whilst the dogged well organised second eleven began to "run rings" around them. Some naughty tackles were inflicted on the second team forwards, and given the presence of a good referee, this activity would in all probability have been "nipped in the bud". Regrettably however and as the match was a "friendly", no authorised officials were requested, and the game was refereed by the self-appointed Mr Leonard Lippa, Chairman of the football club management committee, who probably had never refereed a game in his life. Probably never played football either. His remedy for the increasing preponderance of niggly fouls on the second team was to give somewhat avuncular pleas to the perpetrators… "now come on lads; it's only a friendly…" which naturally were ignored. The second eleven maintained their discipline in the teeth of increasing provocation and were rewarded a little before half time with a second goal. Then it happened, and Fastovski's worst nightmare ensued; the dreaded clash between the Brothers Moss. With the imminent arrival of half time, Ronnie and Laurie went for a high ball which resulted in the two shoving each other somewhat, posturing a lot but without actually coming to blows. On witnessing this, Marshal Klein deserted his command post (a "Court Martial Marshal" offence if ever there was one) and ran down the field to join in the coming battle, pursued by a huffing and puffing short corpulent middle aged Lennie Lippa who aware of the potential danger in the situation felt obliged to assert his "authority". The immediate danger however was averted by both teams quickly separating the brothers who seemed quite co-operative. The arrival of a now confused and anxious Lennie Lippa created the "Gotterdammerung" which had always seemed likely, and puffing himself up like "the croaking bullfrog of the Tontine Marsh" as had Churchill so famously described Mussolini (who in effect was slightly less pompous than Lennie Lippa;) thereby set in motion the inevitable Twilight of the Gods, by ordering Ronnie Moss off the field. Ronnie's "Red mists" by comparison put Marshall Kleins variety into the category of "Pink blancmange" and his ordering off resulted into his shaking like a volcano whilst a thrill of horror spread through the players aware that they were about to witness an eruption of Krakatoan intensity. Protests by some of the players at the severity of the sending off were forestalled by the sudden explosion of wrath by Ronnie; who struck Mr Lippa full on the jaw; literally "poleaxing" the unfortunate prone onto the pitch… to be followed on the instant (and on Mr Lippa too) by Ronnie who had now swelled into a monstrous giant slobbering frothing murderous baby; bashing his fists like piledrivers as an enraged child would do on the carpet… This particular baby however, (and in the absence of a carpet), was ministering his tantrum directly onto the unfortunate Mr Lippa who was by now lying completely still with something of a grin on his face and clearly in a state of catatonic shock. Or something like that. They were quickly joined on the ground by the muscular and powerful Hindenburg who had placed Ronnie in a strangling reverse head lock; hard round the wind pipe, but was completely unable to move him whilst the battering and frothing gained in intensity and while more and more of the boys joined in the scrum endeavouring to separate Lippa from the fate of inverse infanticide which now seemed imminent. Surveyors of which both "Slag Heap" and "Cake" were eventual practitioners would have recognised that from the side elevation there was now little or no sight of Lippa whatsoever, as the combined weight and blows of Ronnie (plus the increasing scrum) had pushed him quite well beneath the sodden surface of the pitch, fixed grin and all…in fact he appeared somewhat like a steamrollered character in another cartoon; which invariably would follow "Ming the Merciless" at the News Theatre in Clayton Square. Laurie looked on this scene starring his brother with some apparent indifference, as no doubt he had seen this sort of thing before, but it certainly looked to everybody else that they were witnessing a murder…no less.

At this juncture, Fastovski in endeavouring to use his "captains influence" stood over the deranged centre forward, and in somewhat of an imperious gesture of unconscious irony demanded that he "let go this instant, failing which, I must warn you that you will be reported to the football Management Committee" forgetting for the moment that the man being buried alive beneath the grotesque baby was in fact the Chairman of that august and holy institution. The match was abandoned.

Ronnie left Liverpool a little while later to be seen on one occasion by Fastovski and Cake Wassermann in Willesden. Laurie went to the States to seek his fortune and was never heard of again. Marshall Klein became Lord Mayor of Liverpool for the millennium year 2000. Fastovski was promoted to the first team and later decamped to the

London School of Economics, and Mr Lippa survived, with however something of a fixed grin which accompanied him thereafter.

...AND 58 YEARS LATER!!

INCORPORATING JEWISH GAZETTE   VOL 84 NO 1

Friday, March 21, 2014 ▓ Adar Sheni 19, 5774   Founded in 1950 by Frank and Vivienne Harris

Merseysiders walk off pitch in ref storm

BY JASON STEIN

LIVERPOOL Haroldeans have almost certainly handed the Manchester Jewish Soccer League to Manchester Maccabi 2nd after sensationally walking off the pitch against Maccabi's third team on Sunday.

Grandma Lena with Tilly and Morris

Uncle Dave (In pensive vein)

Uncle Joe (In 'Hirohito' Pose)

Uncle Morris Conscription photo 1939

Chapter Seven
Warrior Avyn

Fastovski was in a fairly foul mood that morning. He had wasted two precious hours in a photographic studio whilst prancing around like Kate Moss in drag. The resultant "works of art" were well below his expectations; were completely unsuitable as publicity material (which had been the original intention) and he was completely exhausted, to boot. In circumstances such as these, the only recourse was to Pam's Café for some strong Assam, followed by further strong Assam. Detailing the calamity to Pam, and Harry "take no prisoners" Chapman (Consultant at the nearby Royal Free Hospital) ameliorated his agony somewhat, and the strengthening, fortifying and spirit-raising qualities of Pam's tea eventually restored his good humour, but nevertheless, a bit too soon for his liking. Happily, his former discomfiture was quickly restored however on the entrance of "Charteris" she of the cut-glass accent, and cheery toothsome smile who, espying Fastovski scowling in the corner and seemingly oblivious to the lowering look he gave her decided to join him at his table. He actually liked Charteris who was a "jolly good chap" with antecedents somewhere British Raj, and probably some fine cavalry regiment (maybe even Hodson's Horse at Poona…who knows), but one needed energy to withstand her; which at the moment he lacked. She also had in tow her granddaughter of three who if anything exceeded Charteris in loquacity, and with whom she joined in the verbal investment of Fortress Fastovski, siege guns and all whilst the besieged unfortunate searched in his trouser pocket for a white handkerchief as a gesture of unconditional surrender in a desperate attempt to achieve the inner redoubt of his mind and shut out the shells and mortars of their "yakkety yak" which were raining down on him unremittingly from a great height…

Liverpool May 1941 and the two-year-old Fastovski was listening to the bombs raining down from the circling German bombers, and regarding from the security of his pram the flashes and eruptions in the starlit sky, and the thump thump from the "ack-ack" at Sefton Park on which his dad Issy was soon to serve so wonderfully ineffectually. He had been alerted to the imminent raid only minutes before by the air raid sirens which had opened up with their banshee wail of approaching death to be followed by the familiar droning of the throbbing engines gaining in intensity as they flew in to be met by the distant crump of anti-aircraft fire on the outskirts of the heroic city, which was about to "take it". His mother moved the pram under the stairs (which could offer some protection in the event of a direct hit), to be cajoled into a game of "peek-a-boo" by his grandmother Nechamka much against his will and to his annoyance, but nevertheless he had little option other than to suffer the ensuing "yakkety yak" delivered in a mixture of Russian/Yiddish and a Liverpool variant of English, accompanied by the equal annoyance of falling bombs.

Fastovski's memories of the May Blitz were etched deeply into his psyche, and which despite his tender years he both observed, and understood in complete clarity. Having spoken quite fluently just after his first birthday, and possessed with the facility of curiosity, he conversed comfortably with his family about the events. On another night and having had installed in the "parlour" a Morrison Shelter, Fastovski and his father were attempting some sleep, listening to the bombs coming closer, and watching the searchlights lighting up the starlit sky. Fastovski was concerned about his mother who had refused to join them but was abed upstairs. The young shaver felt it his duty to leave the security of the iron open-sided shelter, to climb the stairs in the dark and urge his mother to safety downstairs. He found her with the lights on (but with the curtains drawn, according to regulations) and reading a book. Refusing his suggestion that she join him and Issy, she explained that if one's name was on the bomb there was nothing to be done and that she preferred to read her book…the exchange was conducted in a quite matter of fact way whilst bombs were exploding nearby. A day or so later, Tilly had taken her offspring for afternoon tea on the sixth floor of the giant "Lewis's" Department Store in the City Centre. They were joined by her mother Lena, and her good friend Mrs Shure, her daughter Ethel and jolly four-year-old granddaughter Sylvia who some years later married Joey de Cordova, brilliant singer, close friend of Jimmy Tarbuck and protégée of Issy, and who died tragically of tuberculosis before his thirtieth birthday. Afternoon tea of cakes and sandwiches were being served on the ornate cake stands, by chatty and smartly attired waitresses, accompanied by pots of tea or coffee. Tinned fruit salad followed accompanied by synthetic cream. The café was crowded and the happy clientele were being entertained by the Ronnie O'Dell Band playing jazz standards, with the soon-to-be famous Bruce Trent singing, whilst playing the Double Bass and wearing a good American style loose fitting light coloured suit and snazzy tie (as did all the band) which was set off by his dark glasses.

Fastovski was absolutely captivated by the whole thing...the café...the band...the elegant ambience...the flirty waitresses...the jazz...everything. The band was London based but were doing a residency at Lewis's and were staying in a flat in the Kensington District of Liverpool not far from Lena who shared her large rambling house with her musician sons Joe and Dave. The youngest son Morris had been conscripted on the outbreak of war, had served in the Welch Regiment in Dempseys Second Army, and was killed at the bloody battle of Reichwald Forest in Germany on February 25 1945 the last major battle of the whole campaign. He is buried in a small and cosy graveyard in Uden. When Fastovski visited it many years later, he found that his grave had been vandalised. In his last letter home, he had asked Fastovski to learn the words of the new hit song "swing on a star" and sing it to him on his return. Fastovski learned the song...

On leaving the café, Tilly remarked to her young son that if there was one place in Liverpool that she would definitely feel safe, it would be right there in Lewis's Department Store. Fate decreed otherwise however, and that very night the store received a pounding and was virtually destroyed. The sky was ablaze with fire that night as a very

121

relaxed Tilly and Issy casually wheeled Fastovski in his pram into Sefton Park to the nearest air raid shelter located on the Triangle Field. Young Fastovski marvelled at the beauty of the blood red and black sky, and the green emitted from the flashes of the explosions and overheard his parents remarking on the calamity that had befallen Lewis's. Later that night, an ammunition ship laden with 1,000 tons of explosive received a direct hit, destroying Huskisson Dock, remarkably with only four killed…but Liverpool shook. Elsewhere people died in their hundreds, some no doubt humming the current hit song "I don't want to set the world on fire"…

Lena Green of the lustrous copper hair and dark green piercing eyes had, in 1905 arrived unaccompanied in Liverpool from a small town near Riga in Latvia; in transit to New York where she was awaited by her fiancée who had sent her money for the passage. At the Liverpool Dock, she was examined by the Port Health Authority and was referred to a specialist in Glasgow for suspected glaucoma. There she met Wolf Brown and fell pregnant with her first-born John Joseph Brown. They lived in the slums of the dreaded Gorbals and where a year later, their second son David was born. Two years later, they moved to Liverpool where Tilly and later Morris was born. They settled in the predominantly Jewish Brownlow Hill district where the children attended Pleasant Street School and where in the next road the Fastovski/Feldmans lived. Lena had a strange dark side. She had told the young Fastovski that as a young girl in Latvia she had "drowned" in a river and had actually died. She knew and "felt" the life in trees which she loved with a passion. She dwelt now and again with young Fastovski on her pity and sorrow at the dreadful death of Jesus which seemed to preoccupy her on occasion, and subliminally perhaps instilled in her young grandchild his later awareness of the betrayal of this heroic Jewish King and freedom fighter for Israel by the propagandists of the Gentile Christian Church; the greatest calumny in the whole of history, and perpetrated later by the Romans the true murderers of "God". Jesus too (like Lena) was portrayed in the earliest depictions of him as copper haired and green eyed as indeed were her father, three brothers and her sister. Whether she was aware of this or not was never revealed. Fastovski's daughter Rachel with the flaxen hair of the Feldmans had at the age of eight developed an infatuation with the death of Thomas á Becket when he had related the story to her whilst she sat on his knee in the nave at Canterbury Cathedral, and would cry in his memory and wanting his hat. Fastovski passed on to her his feelings for Jesus, his enduring love of Israel and unyielding commitment to Zionism. They would sing together the marching songs of the Palmach freedom fighters and the stirring lyrics of the Jewish Pioneers draining the malarial swamps of the Galilee. They would sing the raucous cockney songs of the old East-end together and all the Christian hymns and Carols at Christmas, which they both loved. Like her father she was a fine pianist and possessed also of a beautiful top soprano voice. She spent time in Israel on a Kibbutz and learned to speak Hebrew fluently.

When Rachel was ten years old, and when Fastovski was suffering a nervous breakdown from the strains of a breaking marriage, she helped rally him with the musical "Annie" and the song "The sun will come out to-morrow".

Dave Brown was a talented professional dance band musician, who had appeared in the Noel Thoms Orchestra in one of the first BBC live outside broadcasts, which was relayed from the Grand Hotel in Port Rush. Back home in Liverpool, Lena (his mother) kept "open house" for the vast array of pals that her children had, and including many ot the local and visiting musicians on the dance band/jazz circuit. The famous trumpeter Nat Gonella, was an occasional visitor as was his brother "Bruts" who would visit more frequently due no doubt to his interest in Dave's sister Tilly. Dave played Saxes and clarinet, and also violin which was the fashion in the evolution of that particular form of music from the 1920s into the 1930s. He was very handsome with "chiselled features" fair hair and blue eyes, (looking very much like the young George C Scott;) and had made a conquest of, and later married the lovely Trudi Jones, the boss's daughter of the large tailoring factory where his brother Joe and he had worked. The Jones were a lovely, impeccably mannered old Welsh family who lived in a beautiful old house in sedate Allerton with a magical rose garden where Mr Jones would attend to them with his secateurs whilst speaking liltingly in that wonderful Welsh cadence to young Fastovski. Joe had musical enthusiasm but no talent whatsoever, and for which he compensated by playing virtually everything with the same level of enthusiasm and exceedingly badly. Young Fastovski would keep the family highly amused by his impersonation at the piano of his Uncle Joe in his infamous rendition of "Whispering". As Tilly was fond of relating, Joe could empty a room with two chords on a banjo and one note on the double bass. Joe looked very much like his father, with strong Oriental appearance (as indeed had some of the Fastovski's), and during the war his passing likeness to the Emperor Hirohito of Japan; whilst not causing his arrest would often be regarded with some amusement.

On the afternoon that Fastovski had taken his wife and daughter to Canterbury, he had popped into a shop which traded in 1920/1930s ephemera, fashions and music, whilst his wife took Rachel for an ice-cream a little way up the street. His eye was drawn to a picture postcard from 1930 picturing the ballroom of the Grand Hotel, Port Rush from where his Uncle Dave had broadcast in that very year. Whilst looking at it, the background music of pre-war recordings in the shop changed to "The music goes round and round" which Dave loved, and years before his early death from tuberculosis would often sing or hum to himself. Fastovski found a strange sensation overcoming him as if he and Dave were in the same room. He moved a little unsteadily into the street, with his breath tightening a little; where he met his wife and daughter and to whom he related this most moving episode. His wife shrugged and looked away.

The Jones in a certain way represented a peripheral but emotionally cohesive component to the young Fastovski, as a result of their "Welshness". North Wales is only some twenty miles from the great Port and as a consequence Liverpudlians in general would spend a lot of time in that beautiful and mystical land where the people spoke with poetry in their hearts and music in their soul. Terrible beer though…and much worse than the Liverpool "Higson's" and

"Threllies" which Fastovski would avoid at all costs. The only beer that exceeded the above in awfulness was foisted upon Fastovski when on entering for the first time the "Three Tuns Bar" at the London School of Economics somebody bought him a pint of hideously weak and tasteless "Fremlin's Ale", half inch of sediment and all. This naturally met Fastovski's criteria for "savage irony" and thereafter during three dissolute years in the "Red Rat Hole" (By which the London School of Economics was widely known), he would drink no other. In a sense, Fastovski had little choice in the matter, as having seen an ad on the student union notice board concerning the formation of a trad band, he turned up and was accepted as pianist.

Friday night was trad night at the "Three Tuns" where Fastovski and the band were plied by friends and admirers alike, with the perceived currency of "Fremlin's". It would have been considered extremely rude to turn down the accelerating conveyor belt of drink with the result that the boys would invariably end up somewhat inebriated and with "Doctor Jazz" sounding a bit like "Come into the garden Maude"… On such a night, the boys repaired to Soho for a meal, and passing the famed Cy Laurie Club, went in to listen to his band which was playing much of the repertoire of the "Three Tuns Stompers". The eminent LSE "kapellmeister" and trumpeter Eddie Matthews (who later became a Prison Governor "somewhere in the Midlands") invited the great Cy to let Fastovski "sit in" for a number or two…and to which he surprisingly agreed. He did a couple of numbers which seemed OK and was invited back on a number of occasions.

When Fastovski was four years of age, he was found to have infected tonsils and adenoids and his parents opted to have the operation performed by the consulting specialist Mr Bernstein privately at a clinic in Woolton, Liverpool. He was rendered unconscious by the old-fashioned chloroform mask whilst being held down by the nurses during his struggles, through which he kept seeing an image of a skull, and the face of a horned bull alternately moving towards him and moving away again. When he awoke, it was to find himself next to a vessel full of his blood next to his bedside; with his parents sitting by his bedside with an ice cream which they had apparently searched all over wartime Liverpool to find. The fastidious young man would resist conversation with any but the prettiest nurses especially a very attractive blonde who he fell madly in love with, and would complain at the cold fried egg which would be served, and seemingly without any attention to it's being crisped the way he liked it. His dad, Issy, regrettably had given instructions not to serve his son bacon; which further compounded the vandalisation and violation of his breakfast. Toast was okay though. On bidding the blonde nurse (but not the strict bespectacled matron) goodbye, he was treated by Tilly and Lena to a visit to "Coopers" the coffee house, which Liverpudlians of a certain age will even now reminisce over with romance in their souls and tears in their eyes.

Coopers was a huge old food store built about 1870 in Church Street Liverpool and facing the equally famous "Bunney's" store built a little later but in the very appealing art nouveau style and which was later pulled down by the consent of the Fascist/Labour criminals of the Liverpool City Council, in the 1970s. Coopers represented everything appertaining to the powerful, beautiful and self-confident Victorian Liverpool which deserved its reputation as the "Second City of the Empire" and which continued until 1956 when coincidentally, the Labour Lunatics pulled down the world famous overhead Electric Railway, the aorta of Liverpool; which had been imported by an enterprising businessman from New York in the 1890s and which traversed the entire length of the fourteen miles of the Liverpool docks…

Liverpool began to die.

The food hall was somewhat like Harrods and stocked every conceivable type of delicacy imaginable for the huge middle class and discerning population.

Food which would not be found normally except in the Grand Hotels of London's West End, or in its earlier years the grandest of them all, the "Adelphi" which being nearby to Coopers received the powerful, connected and wealthy in transit between Liverpool, London and New York. Where the "top brass" would stay and outside of where in a Blackshirt rally in 1936, Oswald Mosley was hit on the head with a brick, hurled (according to Issy, by himself) but a claim shared at one time, it would seem by the entire Jewish and indeed some non-Jewish youth of Liverpool. A visit to the food hall was an experience itself to be savoured and one could smell, and sense the taste of the hanging hams, salamis and smoked meats, the glistening bucklings, bloaters and pale Isle of Man Kippers, the finest fat white veined "middle-cut" smoked salmon, beluga and sevruga caviar, creamy pungent English and continental cheeses, the exotic fruits (such as cumquats, mangoes and Chinese gooseberry) which were the normal fare for the owners of the great mansions that circled Sefton Park with their wide Parisian style avenues. The clear white butter which was hammered into shape by wooden spatulas on the cold marble counter by smartly clad and impeccably groomed and well-mannered gentlemen shop assistants, and then individually wrapped mostly in one pound smartly presented blocks. Huge red metal vats roasted the Brazilian, Colombian, Kenyan and Javan coffees fresh, to be shovelled delicately into dark-salmon coloured cardboard containers adorned with elegant dark blue copper plate writing; whilst the teas sat quietly and less exuberantly alongside with their more esoteric and slightly snooty demeanour in their varieties of Assam, Darjeeling, Ceylon…and Fastovski's favourite by far, the unsurpassable Orange Broken Pekoe. The smells were heavenly a sensory delight which the customers enhanced with their undisguised aura of pleasure in this veritable and venerable Theatre of Culinary Art.

Above the food hall was situated Cooper's Café, which covered the same large area as the food hall below and was modelled on the great State rooms of the luxury liners based in Liverpool such as "White Star", "Blue Funnel" "Cunard"…and "Peninsular and Orient" which did the romantic run to Java, and Surabaya, and the seedy ports of the hidden Pacific. It was a café that lost none of its intimacy despite its discreet opulence and grandeur. There were two rows of about ten tables each, well-spaced and furnished in the dark mahogany Rattan style which graced the well-loved liner "Mauretania". The deeply burnished parquet flooring between each row was covered by deep blue and gold Chinese carpeting which ran the length of the hall. Light and elegant fare such as Scrambled egg on toast,

Welsh Rarebit and Buck Rarebit were served, together with the stylish cake stands stacked delicately with cucumber sandwiches and moist fruit cake chocolate eclairs and tiny rhubarb tarts. Coopers home-baked toasted tea cake dripping with Welsh butter would be served, accompanied again by their own freshly roasted coffee served in elegant EPNS jugs (one for the coffee, the other for the hot milk.) On the table there was real cube sugar, both white and brown…and tongs.

The Coopers "Café Brand" coffee was Colombian; unsurpassed for aroma, smoothness, taste and aftertaste (very important). Better by far, as Fastovski was to learn later than the dreadful bitter French rubbish, and Italian effete excuses for coffee, and the Yankee poison. The only coffee apart from Coopers which appealed in later years to Fastovski was the Dutch variety, adorned with a spiced biscuit and served in the elegant, comfortable and high-quality restaurants and cafés of Amsterdam, Leyden and the Hague. The Cooper waitresses were similarly elegant, pretty and impeccably mannered and attired in the lovely black and white dress uniform which at that time was a symbol of pride to that trade (as indeed was the neat and lust-provoking and sadly missed nurses' uniform of the day). Huge potted palm plants lined both sides of the café, and to cap it all, an impeccably attired string quartet would on occasion be found playing selections of the Light Operetta of von Suppe, Frans Lehar, Imre Kalman, Robert Stoltz and Ivor Novello. On entering this paradise, one's breath would literally be taken away.

At that time, Liverpool abounded in many high class restaurants (eating houses as Fastovski would refer to them) and cafés. Fastovski's parents had rarely introduced him into the world of posh restaurants, but nevertheless would often entertain him to a good meal at places where Issy was well known, and would (certainly in Jackie's Café) be invited into the kitchen to select his choice; accompanied on occasion by his young son. During the dark days of the war, Jackie's Café survived a bombing which destroyed the whole block and left him isolated from much of the surrounding area. "Jackie's" would usually be full, but a table would always be found for Issy, and a good piece of steak (otherwise unobtainable at that time) would materialise on Issy's plate, but discreetly concealed under the vegetables. The steamed sultana pudding and custard that Jackie cooked (no supermarket ready-made rubbish those days) was the very best that Fastovski and family had ever tasted… Into this category also came the Yankee-supplied dried egg in large copper-coloured tins…no omelette ever tasted better.

'Well, I really MUST be going…time DOES fly…it's AWFULLY nice to have seen you again…and catching UP on things…'

Fastovski was in the process of finishing off the omelette which Rashid the manic Berber chef had prepared for him and was ruminatively chewing the last piece of remaining crisp wholemeal toast and butter, when he was jolted back to reality by the cheerful Charteris trumpeting her imminent departure.

He smiled weakly, and uttered a few platitudinous and cliche-ridden sincere sounding sentiments of an anodyne and quite meaningless nature (which seemed to satisfy her) whilst she drew elegantly back from the table whilst urging her fearsome granddaughter to "Say goodbye to the nice gentleman". The child, however, fixed him with a malignant piercing cold stare whilst adopting a tight lipped silent aura of primal aggression; to which Fastovski responded in like vein. This transportation of unvoiced magnitudinous hostility and ill intent went on for some few unblinking moments; to the mutual satisfaction of both combatants, on which they both slowly and carefully drew apart; somewhat like Jake la Motta and Tony Zale at the conclusion of their own notorious boxing bloodbath at Madison Square Garden, "Noo York" in the sweltering hot summer of 1947.

Fastovski shuddered gently and continued his previous reverie, which at this point had been zooming in on the great "Maison Lyons" that huge café/restaurant situated on three floors in the centre of the fashionable Church Street area of Liverpool. This fine establishment (and second only to Coopers) had been rebuilt in the early 1920s in the Art Deco style which was then in vogue. Much art deco building whilst stylish, tended to be shoddily constructed for some reason, and in the adulated "Bauhaus" concept occasionally too sparse and lacking in character and warmth. That ridiculous edifice in Hampstead just around the corner from "Pams Café" was a singular case in point. Situated adjacent to the Georgian Keats Grove, the most elegant part of Hampstead, and in a leafy stylish avenue of large and comfortable Edwardian Houses, the Erno Goldfinger monstrosity "schticken out liken ein zore tumb"…Mein Gott, vat in Himmel did der grosse Dumpkoff haben in mind, hein? Looking something like a "One stop shop" in a South London Sink Estate in Peckham, the daft building should have been pulled down years ago (brick by brick preferably) and replaced with something beautiful, in character with the area…at least it would have had the effect of removing the lunatic middle aged sandal-wearing serious looking and shabby Liberal "uber dope" culture tourists from descending on Fastovski's new territory, gawping admiringly at something they pretended to like and enjoy, and then be relieved of £8 for the privilege.

"Maison Lyons" however was magnificent in every conceivable detail. The overhanging huge suspended lozenge-shaped glass lighting which adorned the ceiling softly sat in various shades of lilac, dark blue and pink; the tables and chairs were made of solid light coloured beech with the "wrap around" backed chairs being upholstered in a coffee coloured soft leather. The floor was laid with blue carpet set off in Egyptian style decorative feature, and a bit like a Miro painting. The walls were encased in the highest quality beechwood…all reminiscent somehow of a film set such as in "Flying down to Rio" starring Fred Astaire and Ginger Rogers. One could almost imagine her breezing in with her tight fitting satin dress, silly little hat (and a "Long Island" fearsome mother in tow…a part perhaps for Marie Dressler?) to be flirted at by a cheeky evening suited Astaire and much to her (apparent) indignation)…Fastovski remembered the delicate little vanilla, or strawberry ices served in a special EPNS plate with an inbuilt receptacle for the tiny exquisite elegant ice, and served with an extremely long delicate spoon, by an equally elegant, pretty and charming waitress.

Some weeks after recovering somewhat from "Charteris's Blitzkrieg", Fastovski was visiting Liverpool and had decided to breakfast at one of the Hotels in the area. This plan of action had been occasioned by an incident the previous day, when upon entering a café in Lark Lane, he had encountered an alien culture of language, speech, manner, deportment, mode of dress, intelligence…and all this from the waitress from whom he had attempted with some great difficulty to negotiate two slices of wholemeal toast accompanied by a pot of tea with skimmed milk. The present waitress in Liverpool (2006) differs somewhat from her charming, pretty, well mannered, properly attired and sociable predecessor of yesteryear seemingly in every conceivable respect, but especially in an occasional tendency to an immense stupidity accompanied by incredible ugliness (at least in the experience of the overtly fastidious Fastovski, who in the case of café service would give little latitude). The white- trainer- adorned- tee- shirt- clad- specimen, with the ring in her fleshy navel; exposed fat bum with tattoo, and dull brutish dead eyed features, and greasy hair pulled tight back in a little knot above the hard neck; had apparently never heard of wholemeal toast. Some gentle educative probing however from Fastovski in the direction of "Brown Bread" did momentarily receive the faintest glimmer of recognition in the piggy eyes of the brute- visaged virago who by bodily gesture and look of annoyance seemed to imply that she knew all along about brown bread but hadn't let on for reasons best known to herself. Her annoyance increased somewhat when he requested "skimmed milk" which evinced a response of uncomprehending defensive antagonism. Fastovski suggested that she ask the manageress…which she did.

The hard faced and petulant manageress (who by appearance may have been the mother of the "young lady") came over to Fastovski to enquire as to what the problem was. It would appear that in treading the six feet between the table and the counter the waitress had forgotten what it was she need ask the manageress, and presumably had instead perhaps indicated that Fastovski was possibly "trying to cause trouble" or something.

'What's the problem!' said the manageress, somewhat aggressively to Fastovski.

'No problem,' responded Fastovski, 'I don't like whole milk, and would prefer skimmed…would you have any?'

'Wegotsemiskimmedmilkisthatorright!' she responded; like a British machine gunner at Ypres, and as if Fastovski had by his question **really** been causing trouble. *'Yerdontwantmuchdooyer,'* she added, in that jocular sarcasm which often passes locally as Scouse "humour". Fastovski had never experienced anything of the kind before, and certainly not at his Club at St James; nor at the discreet Goring Hotel, in Knightsbridge and haunt of the aristocracy and demi-monde, (and himself on occasion)…which now beckoned a.s.a.p.…if not sooner.

The next morning, he was enjoying his walk-through Sefton Park whilst building up a good appetite for his planned poached eggs and trying to erase the horrors of the previous morning. The birds were singing in the trees and the lovely lake was rippling gently under the white-skinned shimmering Palm House; one of the joys of this majestic area. Entrance to the hotel necessitated the ringing of the doorbell which was answered (eventually) and surprisingly by none other than Wayne Rooney himself. Closer inspection however revealed that that it was not in fact Wayne Rooney himself the famous footballer, but the (female) receptionist herself who bore an uncanny resemblance to himself in facial features, bulldog build and close cropped haircut. 'Yeah?' she enquired, suspiciously.

'Could I have breakfast please?' responded Fastovski, adding that he was not resident.

'In dere,' she responded nodding vaguely in the direction of the dining room. He seemed to be the only diner. In the process of sitting down and settling into the letters page of his "Daily Telegraph' which he had brought with him, he found himself being shouted at by the Rooney "doppelganger" standing half in and half out the door.

'Pardon?' responded Fastovski, somewhat taken aback.

'*WORYERAVIN*!' she demanded testily. Needless to say, there was neither wholemeal toast nor skimmed milk.

Wendy with Tilly – Southport 2012

Fastovski with girlfriend Wendy 2007

Chapter Eight
Popper's Private Army

Fastovski knew Frank Judge quite well. It was during the time that Fastovski held a well-paid position in an old family firm in the London "Square Mile". Frank was an older man, who had led a very interesting war-time career as a member of "Popski's Private Army" in the dunes of North Africa. Friendly, outgoing and modest, he nevertheless had an outrageous sense of humour, and (to his credit) would never talk about his exploits except of course when it suited him, or when he was in the company of friends, or plied with drink, or whatever seeming combination of the aforementioned seemed appropriate at the time. He was marvellous company, a good pal and a true human being who helped Fastovski "out of a scrape" on one career-threatening occasion. The Popski personnel all shared the same personality profile, as individualistic spirits who could never fit into the mould of regimental discipline, but were resourceful and of a brave and adventurous/reckless disposition which suited their tactics as an independent reconnaissance and strike force deep within the German and Italian lines in Libya. Smiling cutthroats with a liking for gin and tonic would be the best description.

Popper was in some regard similar to Popski in that he built around him a cadre of young fanatical adherents who would stop at nothing in the pursuit of their leader's diktats, and seemingly, whatever the consequences. Whilst Popski however was a "Warrior of the Desert"; Popper (as a cushioned comfortable Professor at the London School of Economics) was more a "Warrior of the *Dessert"* (accompanied by a good Chablis or possibly a fine Speitleser Rheisling now and again). His day job however as Professor of Logic and Scientific method had earned him world renown as one of the foremost and radical philosophers of the age. Fastovski as a student in the Department of International Relations had no occasion to meet Popper academically or socially, but would nevertheless have something of an illicit arrangement with Mrs Popper most afternoons, when the great Professor would usually be giving his classes to (amongst others the trombone player in the jazz band…a crashing bore incidentally and an awful trombonist…absolutely perfect of course for New Orleans, but less so for Bloomsbury…). Oh yes, Mrs Popper. Well ACTUALLY, although bearing the same patronymic as the illustrious Jewish-Viennese emigre she was not in fact his wife. Indeed, she appeared to be no relation whatsoever to the phamed philosopher. She did, however, run the LSE equivalent of a Viennese Salon in a little room above the Three Tuns Bar, where she would serve tea and cakes. Mrs Poppers Parlour (as it was called) was a haven for those of the Bohemian set who did not drink alcohol (which restricted her customer base somewhat) and for the whimsical/romantic/tea drinking dilettantes who frequented it. As Fastovski in fact straddled both

139

fellowships with consummate ease (and as "Fremlins" ale in his opinion did not strictly qualify as "drinking") he would repair to the bosom of Mrs Popper in enjoyment of the Café Society. The "illicit" nature of Fastovski's relationship with Mrs Popper grew gradually but eventually with some fervour, and it was due mainly to Machiavelli, Renaissance author of "The Prince" which Fastovski found both amusing, and also extremely instructive in his infatuation with the noble art of darts in which he portrayed all the single minded fanaticism of a "Popski" at his best, or worst, whatever. You see in those days of yore, licensing laws were rigorously enforced, and afternoons were reserved in the main to sleeping off the effect of the morning, in preparation for the abandon of the evening. Mrs Popper however had a discreet arrangement with some of her "boys" when surreptitiously, glasses of lemon tea would alchemise themselves into a bottled beer ("India Pale Ale" usually)…and the secret was well kept on pain of death, or even worse.

Quite understandable and quite illicit…nein?

Soon after his enlisting in the jazz band (The LSE Stompers) Fastovski soon drew, and was in turn drawn into that circle of gross eccentrics…err…close friends with whom he would share a social life veering from the adequately disgraceful to the mere adequate; a scenario which to his recall was rarely played out in the academic cloisters of class or lecture…which would have been considered too "keen"…you get the picture no doubt. By some sort of strange osmosis most of his pals gravitated to the dart board situated at the end of the Bar, in which Fastovski also, was eventually drawn. His possession of excellent hand/eye coordination, was however not satisfied initially by the somewhat repetitious and pointless exercise of throwing needles at cork…until that is one of the more dissolute "Old Guard" at the bar, Codrington-Ball; explained the game of "Killer", and Fastovski was "hooked", or more properly "impaled"

In short, the game of "Killer" was based on each participant being given a number (including the double, and treble)…comprising "Three lives"; with the object of the game being to knock out all the others by the use of shifting "alliances" and "understandings" with the other participants which could be broken "accidentally" (many apologies!! Oh dear I assure you it was an accident. It won't happen again…you…er…won't go for me… will you"?) or betrayed with open savage glee as befitted the nastiness of the moment. A game of "Killer" would invariably end with greater bloodshed than at the Battles of Borodino or Magenta, with battered ego's broken friendships and exhaustion of mind and spirit. In short, the playing out on the dartboard of the principles of Machiavelli which as an avid student of International Relations suited Fastovski perfectly, even more so in fact. In such an environment where one threw one's next dart at the very person with whom one had made a "treaty" against a third party, it was of fundamental importance that one's archery was very accurate; as any miss could immediately expose the jugular of the betrayer to mortal danger from "friend" and foe alike. Fastovski fortunately was very accurate, and rarely suffered divine or any other retribution in this ordeal of despair, and exultation, and generally would exit over dead bodies in his wake. Years later in fact, in the fastnesses of the "Rockie

141

Mountains" he had been accorded the sobriquet of "El hacheta" (hatchet man) by some Italian colleagues, for his skill in throwing the hatchet "Red Indian Fashion". He could hit his target over 25 yards or more, as frequently as Codrington-Ball could drown his epiglottis in "Fremlins" whilst standing stationary at the bar.

On first entering the hallowed portals of the infamous institution (there had two years previously been a student "uprising" over the poor standard of food at the Refectory…appropriate training for that singular form of 1950s student radicalism with the LSE "stamp")…Fastovski in his first act of presence had repaired to the cloistered and sacred Shaw Library and played "Foggy day in London Town" on both the Bechstein and Steinway concert grands which stood like twin altars to the memory of Sidney and Beatrice Webb; founders of the hallowed institution, and whose portrait hung like a pathetic nursery-style-chocolate-box-whistler-derivative. A ridiculous portrait of an insufferably pompous and self-regarding couple which was the object of much (and deserved) amusement, loathing and contempt from the student fraternity…and much credit of course to the artist who had captured the essence of the prim Fabian fanatics. Having thus placed his "spore" as it were on the pianos and entire Institution thereby, the young man registered in the Department of International Relations under Dr Frances Northedge; who would later earn Fastovski's scorn with a gratuitously offensive remark on the "archaic and complex English" that he considered the young student would employ in his essays. No doubt "Frances" Northedge (a man incidentally, but spelling his name the woman's way) would have entertained the same thick-headed view of

Machiavelli's classical Italian. Nevertheless, Fastovski enjoyed the world of intrigue, and the pirouetting gavotte of international diplomacy with all its elements of romance, danger and excitement that personified the unique flavour of this fascinating course. Most certainly, the unimaginative Dr Northedge could neither understand nor appreciate the concomitant component of those writers such as John Buchan, Joseph Conrad and others who's "archaic and complex" English provided the sinister backdrop to the living theatre of International Relations, and he no doubt would have been better suited to a life as an instructor in woodwork at Woolwich Polytechnic. Members of the faculty were obliged to offer a specialised subject in the course selected from a short list which included "The Manchurian Crisis of 1931" which Fastovski selected with some glee, and with the feeling that it might well fulfil his expectations of the "savage irony" which he so enjoyed. You see, it transpired that hardly anybody studied this course, due both to its seeming irrelevance to the "Brave New World" of the 1950s, and the complex nature of the interplay between the contending parties which took a while to digest. It was known to a select few however that the morose Barlow, a hooligan from Osset studied the course, without any effect whatsoever on his character or temperament. The major points of the whole odd episode, at least in Fastovski's eyes were that Lord Lytton wrote a report on the matter for the League of Nations in 1931, which document forming an integral aspect of the course. Fastovski reasoned that as the League of Nations did not bother to study its content neither should he. Secondly, and of much more importance he learned that Henry Pu Yi, Last Emperor of

China, and puppet Emperor of Manchukuo (Manchuria) under the invading Japanese, would visit the jazz clubs of Shanghai and sing with the band which Lord Lytton appeared not to have done. Fastovski was awarded his degree. Northedge went on to great fame, and to-day his portrait resembling a cross between a more-than-crushed-and-constipated Harold Wilson and an earnest looking Bugs Bunny hangs in close proximity to that of Sydney and Beatrice. Serves him jolly well right.

Student life with its wild parties, pithy witticisms, close (and peripatetic) friendships, and the "fin du siecle" atmosphere of Mrs Poppers parlour and the Three Tuns Bar suited Fastovski very well indeed. In possession of a maximum grant from the generous Liverpool Education authority; he could enjoy the benefits of student life which was the domain of a select two percent student population, as compared with the somewhat less selective 60% in 2006. Scholarship aside; Fastovski made many friendships with the lively pretty intelligent girls who abounded, and who gathered at the great jazz gigs that also abounded both at the LSE itself and at Passfield Hall the student residence. On one occasion after a particularly heavy drinking session with some of his Welsh chums, Fastovski spent the night lying/sleeping on the floor whilst listening to an LP of Dylan Thomas reciting "Under Milk Wood; to be joined unexpectedly by a lady with whom he had not enjoyed the formality of a prior introduction. Perhaps this osmotic induction of the cerebral and carnal "Welshness" of the drunken Dylan Thomas by the happily inebriated Fastovski was the trigger that fired his coming relationship some months later with the astounding Dawn, a dark and luscious Welsh Beauty, full of fun and spirit; who hailed from the Rhondda Valley, and by common consent, the most desirable and sought after woman in the entire institution. Fastovski's parents were aware of his new girlfriend and Issy being under the impression that she was Jewish advised him to marry her. Fastovski advised him that Dawn was not in fact Jewish, and on being told, Issy burst a blood vessel in his left eye.

Of all the diverse variety of nationalities at the LSE, Fastovski got on particularly well with the Hungarians. They had arrived en-masse after the abortive Revolution in the previous year of 1956 and indeed many had taken part. Without exception, they all spoke perfect English, but which they would accent frequently for effect when necessary and generally when in conversation with Fastovski, who, with his defined qualities at mimicry would similarly indulge. A large proportion were Jewish, and survivors as children from the horrors of the Eichman years in Budapest and elsewhere.

Possessed of a wonderful deep sense of Jewish irony which, allied to the Hungarian quality of ruminative enjoyable melancholy so redolent of the Magyar personality, they were a very attractive group of people…robust, sentimental, expansive and with a dynamic sexual quality. A particular friendship was formed by Fastovski with a young louche sophisticate who had hailed from Transylvania, and who would muse on the absurdity of his situation and complex levels of nationality. Transylvania had been stripped away from Hungary after the Great War in the treaty of Trianon in

1923, and incorporated into Roumania. The student, Andrascz Mosecz would ponder whether he was Hungarian-Roumanian, or Roumanian-Hungarian; or some further combination including his Transylvanian status. Added to the permutation would be his Jewish component, which would extend the mathematical possibilities into Einsteinian horizons. During a particularly heavy drinking session one lunch time at the "Three Tuns" accompanied by Danish Blue Cheese rolls, schooners of drambuie (the bar was heavily subsidised and drambuie would cost 9d, in old money), and the famed head shattering "Brother Bung" pickled onions, Andrascz confided to Fastovski that his identity crisis was compounded somewhat by that quirk of fate whereby as a Hungarian, his patronymic would precede has given name. Consequently whilst back in the Land of Vlad, he had always considered he was Mosecz Andrascz; in London he discovered to his horror that he was in reality Andrascz Mosecz, and in consequence it was now clear to him that he had in fact never previously existed. 'The trouble vid you, Volly,' he added to Fastovski after some seemingly deep morbid reflection. 'Is that you are a...Vog' (as if that observation in effect, put the entire matter into context).

'A Vodka? Thank you!' added Codrington-Ball, who had been listening in with characteristic affable befuddlement.

Barry Abrahams was Fastovski's closest pal during his LSE years and was some years later to be his Best Man. Barry being blessed with a somewhat plebeian North London Accent, Fastovski addressed him as

146

"Berry". Somewhat shrunken in appearance, slightly stooped and with a good Jewish nose, and very similar in appearance to Ben Warris the comedian; he compensated with a marvellous personality, witty anecdotal style, and a liking for the outrageous which he and Fastovski would share. Very engaging, kind and warm; with a "Landon" street wise demeanour, he was destined tragically to die just a few years later of a cancer which would eat his whole body. A very good player of "Killer" and constant ally of Fastovski; he would tolerate Fastovski's betrayal of him at the dartboard from time to time with a chuckle and smile. He did however seem actually to enjoy drinking his "Fremlins" which would raise an eyebrow or three in the Three Tuns Bar, and the two pals would often to be found at Mooneys Irish Bar (longest bar in UK) in the Strand, dining off huge chunks of cheddar cheese, Vienna Bread, great slabs of butter, mounds of "Brother Bung" onions and all washed down by pints of black strong draught Guinness served with genius by the famous Connemara barman who bore a distinct resemblance to Popeye the Sailorman, and who Fastovski insisted upon calling "Taffy". Fastovski moved in with Barry and his mum Pat, and younger brother and sister in the family flat over Pat's dress shop in Chamberlayne Road, Willesden. Barry's dad had been killed in the war. Having been brought up in the traditional Jewish kosher atmosphere of his parents; Fastovski was somewhat nonplussed at being presented with a pork joint by Pat at his first family Sunday lunch. Learning that Barry had somewhere acquired a driving licence, Fastovski suggested to his pal that they buy a car, and Barry could teach him to drive. In the "Exchange and Mart" they saw reference to a 1933 Ford 8, at Baker Street, described as "being good for its year" and with an asking price of £30. Barry rang the number to be greeted by the exceedingly posh accent of a young lady who made an appointment for them with a Mr Raymond Gottlar, Managing Director and owner of the vehicle. On arriving it transpired that the location was a gigantic car showroom with a selection of top of the range Ferrari and Alfa Romeo dreamcars, and the young students were ushered through the marble-clad-palm-concealed-pillared-showroom to a massive antique desk behind which sat in resplendent glory the powerful figure of Mr Raymond Gottlar smoking a huge cigar. Attired in the finest dogtooth double breasted grey suit, offset with a pale lavender silk shirt and tie of a slightly darker hue, in his buttonhole he was sporting a white carnation, and exuded an excellent aftershave from the sleek rather fleshy middle aged face of a man in his mid-forties, whose thick black hair was brushed back flat and shining with brilliantine. "What can I do for you?" he offered in a booming, exaggerated and ironic posh accent, to the young men, who themselves perhaps mistakenly had omitted to dress for the occasion. 'We've come about the car…the Ford 8…this is the right place?' they responded with a little hesitancy. Gottlar explained that the Ford was kept in a garage at the back of the building, for reasons which he advised yawningly were "perfectly obvious" and took the somewhat overawed boys himself to see the car which turned out to be in good condition with a nice shine, and a good chuntering engine which started "on the button!" On returning to the show room, Gottlar suddenly changed his demeanour from avuncular friendliness to an assumed if insincere tone of quiet menace… "You do both have driving Licences? Or maybe you don't…hmnnn?" Barry hastily produced the document (which he was not obliged to do) and which occasioned a good natured chuckle from the Film Noir Jewish Gangster, and a nervous laugh from the boys. Fastovski explained that they liked the car, but as students, the price would (gulp) be beyond their means.

'Beyond your means,' responded Gottlar with transparently insincere exasperation, and somewhat affected pained boredom…

'Well, if you can't raise thirty quid between you, I suppose you'd better have it for twenty.' He sighed. What style…

In driving the car, it was soon obvious that Fastovsksi lacked not only the hand/eye and (in this instance) feet coordination that he exhibited so skilfully in throwing darts or hatchets, but also the usual caution one would expect from a novice navigating the deadly West End traffic of the great Metropolis. Soon he was referred to by his other great pal "Wild Jim" as "Toad" and for very good reason. You see, Fastovski would drive very fast and in a rather careless manner, and would tend to disregard the strictures of observing the central white line in the road, much to the exasperation of "Berry" who by comparison drove in a sensible law-abiding way. On one occasion whilst returning from a party at Chelsea; given by some of the minor aristocracy with whom he was slightly acquainted through Codrington-Ball; Fastovski was driving (in his usual manner) down a darkened and deserted street at 3am when ahead of him he made out two figures in the gloom

149

beckoning him to stop; which he did. 'Good evening, sir' said the first policeman, 'are you aware that you are driving down a one-way street, and also on the wrong side of the Road.'

'Oh dear me,' responded Fastovski, 'I had no idea…I err…won't do it again I can assure you officer.'

'Not only that, sir,' added the second officer of the Law, 'but we calculate that you were probably doing about fifty miles per hour in a thirty mile per hour zone…have you been drinking, sir?'

'Oh my gosh, I don't think so,' responded Fastovski, 'who was then offered an invitation to step outside the car, and to produce a driving licence. Fastovski responded that as a learner driver he did not possess a driving licence, and had forgotten for some reason he could not remember to display his red L plate which was a legal necessity. Luckily for Fastovski, the two coppers appeared to find the situation so absurd and amusing that they gently advised him to turn around…drive at no more than 28 miles per hour…keep to the left side of the road…don't go over any middle lane… and IF you do get home, sir, do not forget to attach your L Plate to your front bumper…any side will do…' The 1950s were altogether a much gentler age.

Some months later, Fastovski's L plate would become the talk of the London School of Economics. Somebody on the Student Council had suggested a beauty competition for very attractive ladies who frequented its portals, and for which Fastovski's girlfriend Dawn offered to compete. One evening whilst with some friends at a Bar in Bayswater she suggested that Fastovski himself should enter, maintaining that Fastovski's current sporting of a heavy "Viva Zapata" moustache accompanied by a "Van Dyke" beard should not deter his participation. His entry was duly accepted and Martin Dyas a pal from the LSE Drama Society with close theatrical connections, procured for him an early nineteenth century milkmaid outfit with cloth bonnet and smart neat green pinny over the cream-coloured outfit (and a couple of zinc buckets to accompany…they were out of wooden yokes apparently). His entry was accompanied by howls of laughter whilst he lowered the buckets; curtsied demurely to the Judges on the stage, then lowered his gaze shyly whilst raising his skirts slowly to the audience to increasing wolf whistles; only to reveal his L plate securely pinned onto his voluminous underskirts and located strategically to protect his/her modesty. Advancing towards the Judges, Fastovski (who had been introduced under the name "Greasy Fields") gave Gerard Hoffnung, the famous German Jewish eccentric musician/raconteur a peck on the cheek, whilst he bellowed with laughter. Fastovski then approached the second Judge, Digby Wolfe, the famous cabaret artiste who pulled Fastovski onto his knee and held him tight around the waist with further laughter from the audience. The problem (for Fastovski) was that Wolfe was reluctant to let go, and their disengagement was affected only with some visible degree of reluctance by Wolfe. It was only at the reception after the event that it was put around (in whispers those days!) that Digby was a well-known…ermm…hmmn…err…best not talk about it old boy etc, etc.

James Peter Somerville Hardwicke and Fastovski hung around with each other a great deal and later shared a flat ("Pad" as it was known then), together with "Gibbo" an old pal from Liverpool; who by the age of twenty had lost most of his teeth and hair, and who Fastovski would greet by playing "Silver threads amongst the gold" on his entering the Three Tuns for the Friday night jazz "rave"; which the octogenarian teenager would accept with some commendable equanimity. Claiming descent from the famed Bess of Hardwicke of Hardwicke Hall, "Wild Jim's" background was a little less grand and related to a small terrace house in Sheffield which he shared with his mother (he seemed never to mention his father) and an Uncle Percy who he described as an ancient amiable parlour-corner-sitting dependent of indeterminate age, inherited many years before from someone else in the family. The archetypal brooding "angry young man" of the 1950s, he possessed dark smouldering film star gypsy looks concealed within a deep scowl which he would greet anybody and everybody save a few close friends. He professed scorn for inane small talk and for the tittle tattle of women in which he feared he would be obliged to indulge unless it could all be avoided. Nevertheless, he was quickly targeted by the girls in Fastovski's social circle and elsewhere, and was soon to succumb to the "preposterous absurdity" as he would refer to it. The Jewish girls in particular were driven to him, Barry's girlfriend Susan in particular and much to Barry's annoyance who considered that Jim had betrayed him. Given to scornful disregard for most things, Jim would on occasion scatter coin along the pavements of the West End whilst loudly exhorting the pedestrian "Swine and Pigs" to "Gather up the filthy lucre". His friendship with Fastovski was to a large extent based not only on a commonality of viewpoint, but very much on his friend's ability to make him laugh at himself, and to recognise his own eccentricities. On one occasion, Jim's mother sent him a food parcel from Sheffield, comprising a block of unpacked Wensleydale Cheese and some loose pickled walnuts all wrapped clammily in a newspaper in string with a scrawled note referring him to an article he should read therein.

The student life of the 1950s was in many regards apolitical, and college life was based on an unadulterated hedonism accompanied with some study. The profile today (2006) would suggest an even-greater indulgence in hedonistic activity fuelled by intense, and often fanatical political activity fuelled by the fascism of political correctness. Perhaps with some unconscious prescience Fastovski and his pal Palevski recognised this in their forming the so called "Beth Din Department of Jewish Conformity", which consisted solely of Fastovski and Palevski who's role was to monitor conversations, publications and meetings in order to ensure that nothing offensive to Judaism was spoken or written. The inspiration for this intentionally grotesquely humorous concept was a meeting held in Mrs Poppers Parlour by the L.S.E Jewish Society in which both Fastovski and Palevski were members. They were advised to attend this particular meeting which was to be given by Dayan (Rabbi) Swift, a Judge of the Beth Din Court and Jewish "Big Whig", and well known as an intolerant pedant. The meeting was well attended by a group of students who like Fastovski had in the main come from a traditional and tolerant easy-going background which was, and still is representative Jewishness. Dayan Swift after some discursive remarks on Jewish morality seemed to be inferring indirectly to the lax morals of university life and with a warning not to engage in sexual activity outside of marriage, although the great cleric declined to use the word "sex".

'I have to remind you,' he emphasised whilst wagging his finger and trying to look imposing. 'Any child born out of wedlock is a mamzer (bastard).' The response was shocked indignation generally, manifested in the main by hurt protest by the customarily polite and somewhat deferential students so typical of the fifty's era, and with one or two of the girls in tears.

Worse still, the great Rabbi was like Fastovski a Liverpudlian, and whose daughter Stephanie was very pleasant and "normal". To Fastovski, however, the utterance was a prime example of the most extreme form of Savage Irony in which he would love to indulge himself, and both he and Palevski came to the beleaguered Rabbi's aid by engaging in meaningless polemical argument with some of the more outraged students. Out of this event, the "Beth Din Police" were formed where for some time Fastovski and Palevski's interventions in Jewish meetings evolved into a form of Gogolian "Theatre of the Absurd". Their activities took them also into some of the cultural societies where plays were dissected for subliminal antisemitic content to much amusement; especially so during a rehearsal of "Dance of Death" by the gloomy and wonderful Strindberg from the land where the Jew was as uncommon as a circumcision in Hoxton, and which was heavily censored by the "religious police", for "subliminal texting"...shades of modern political correctness. There would have been little point in "monitoring" the political societies in that Israel-friendly era before 1967. Their ironic prescience has manifested itself however in an entirely unexpected direction now identified as the nightmare of Left/Islamic Fascism; where universal vilification of Israel is now the norm, Jew/American hatred the weapon and the World the target.

This frightening and loathsome phenomenon plays "Killer" for real, but otherwise wouldn't be seen dead in Mrs Poppers parlour, nor jiving with the girls to the strains of the LSE trad band's famous rendition of "Royal Garden Blues"…nor joining the boys and girls at the bar for a friendly, civilised, social, human glass of Fremlins ale. Many years later, the fanatic who beheaded the Jewish journalist Daniel Pearl, had himself been a student at the L.S.E.

It would appear that in addition to Machiavelli's influencing the behaviour of Fastovski; some grotesque spiritual manifestation of God, Gogol, Kafka and Ionesco seemed to permeate the psyche of Palevski. Some years after graduating from the London School of Economics, Fastovsksi to his great amusement learned that Palevski had joined one of the most ultra-religious branches of the Chassidim; complete with the huge fur hat, black kaftan and white gaiters of the calling. He eventually became the Dayan of a Yeshivah, a Jewish Rabbinical College in Stamford Hill, the heartland of Jewish Orthodoxy. No doubt he now numbered amongst his circle of acquaintances his previous protagonist the Scouse Ayatollah; Dayan Swift. On being appraised of this Valhallic episode of savage irony, and in considering the appropriate reaction Fastovski mused to himself that perhaps he might invite Codrington-Ball for a friendly flagon of Fremlins ale when he might be prevailed upon to visit the Yeshivah on some pretext or other and "spill the beans" on their old pal in as subtle and deadly Machiavellian manner as he could muster. Fastovski felt satisfied that such a gesture of overt betrayal would be more than appreciated by Palevski, the unwitting creator of a character possibly matched only by Gogol himself, for its quality both of extreme self-parody and grotesque absurdity, and in some ways synonymous with Gogols famous "Nose" which as is well known departed its owner to create a life of its own in another town (Paris actually, but certainly not Stamford Hill). Joe certainly possessed a nose which seemed to harbour such potential. In such anointed and holy crusade of poetic retribution, certainly "Codders" could not remotely compete with the Italian evil one in the art of doing horrible things to ones friends; with the quaffing of "Fremlins" naturally earning his ultimate allegiance. For that reason, perhaps, or possibly because of some flickering of conscience; or maybe because "Codders" couldn't be prised away from the bar, Fastovski withheld his deadly hatchet of dispassionate justice, and the dastardly plan was stillborn; much like the resolution of the Manchurian Crisis of 1931. Nevertheless, in some measure of compensation for his ultimate failure of will at this testing time in the history of Literature and in the interplay of International Relations, Fastovski considered that "Codders" the old Bar-barian would no doubt have crushed Machiavelli soundly in a game of "Killer"; which when passably sober Codrington-Ball was certainly without peer, except of course for Fastovski... sober or otherwise.

As Andrasz Mosecz might have said, 'The slings and arrows of inrageous fivetune.'

Beauty – what a drag

SIR – As a survivor of a previous beauty contest at the London School of Economics, I should advise you that this year's event (report, December 4) is not entirely without precedent.

In 1958, I entered Miss LSE, dressed in drag, sporting a beard and with an "L" plate protecting my modesty. It was judged by the cabaret artist Digby Wolfe and the eccentric raconteur and musician Gerard Hoffnung. I did not win.

Wallace Fields
Liverpool

"Daily Telegraph"
Dec 5 2007

Kappelmeister Eddie Matthews (Trumpet) Fastovski (Piano –
Seated) London School of Economics, Old Theatre September
1957 Formation of the "Three Tuns Stompers"

(L) with 'Boys in the Band'
and
Lady owner of Marlin
sports car

(L) at Glyfada Wine
Festival, Athens
1958

Fastovski strangles Marshal Klein, Wild Jim restrains Fastovski

Closing time at the "Three Tuns"
Codrington Ball (L) Fastovski (C) Wild Jim (R)

Chapter Nine
Ward

David lay dying. Inert in the next bed, Fastovski wasn't feeling too good either. In the general ward of the disgusting "krankenhaus" in Romford where Fastovski had been rushed with a suspected heart attack, he had now spent the better part of ten days undergoing tests, and it was finally decided that he should be transferred to another hospital to undertake an exploratory angiogram. What could be ascertained, was that he had not actually suffered a heart attack, but an episode of unstable angina from which he had suffered since the breakup of his marriage, and which had necessitated emergency admissions on three separate occasions to the same hospital within a matter of the past few weeks. A previous diagnosis some months earlier at the specialist unit at the Royal Brampton Hospital (where he had undergone the dreadful "nuclear" test) produced a rather testy letter back to the GP who had referred him; which stated that Fastovski's heart and arteries were perfectly healthy and the likelihood of his suffering from any heart condition in the future was virtually nil.

David opened his eyes later in the evening, and it appeared that he had stabilised somewhat and was able to speak a little weakly to Fastovski who was listening surreptitiously to Radio 4 on his mobile phone beneath the bedclothes…definitely ***verboten*** in such penal colonies of the National Health Service. It was not easy to understand David for a variety of reasons, and primarily because he was an Iranian, and spoke very little English. He was also quite startling in appearance. Like a lot of Iranians he had quite mad black staring eyes, but was unusually tall and thin with a genuine "Tony Curtis" haircut straight out of the1950s and would brag about his "girlfriends". Most startling thing about him was that whilst an Iranian, he was not in fact a Muslim…but Episcopalian. Most odd. Normally one would expect an indigenous non-Muslim to express himself in the generic rather than the particular; thus "Christian" "Buddhist" "Hindoo". But Episcopalian? Not only that; he also claimed to be a trainee Episcopalian Priest. He appeared to be an asylum seeker of some sort, together with his father who on his visits would tell Fastovski that he had lost his passport (together with three hundred pounds, and false teeth) at Heathrow Airport. Fastovski would explain that regrettably he was not in the position to replace any of the aforementioned commodities, not even to Episcopalians.

Fastovski (who suffered fools and most other people quite badly) had learned to deflect the mad -eyed-linguistically-challenged -teddy-boy-Irano-Episcopalian by pronouncing his verbal ramblings into two categories; "ees good" or alternatively "ees **no** good" which David seemed to appreciate, satisfy his need to communicate with somebody, and (for Fastovski's peace of mind) stop him in his tracks.

Fastovski had been placed in the small four bed male ward by the shuffling "Black Mamma" orderly who seemed to be one of the few personnel with any competence and authority in the entire building. She also liked Fastovski and moved him out of the general ward after he had suffered two consecutive angina attacks, and, being ignored by the staff, was becoming very distressed and hyperventing. She was a committed Christian and on one occasion said prayers over David... "Oh Lard..." and invited Fastovski to join in which he did with the beautiful Jewish prayer of affirmation of life and for those approaching death; the "Shemah", which he solemnly and sincerely pronounced both for David and also himself (just in case). Fastovski felt the majesty and compassion of his Judaism in which the old Jamaican orderly and David were also drawn.

Happily, David did recover. Fastovski's admiration for the elderly Jamaican orderly grew in leaps and bounds over the next week or so in the little annexe where he felt protected by her marvellous presence. Many years before in reading "The Reason Why" by Cecil Woodham Smith the best account of the Crimean War; one brief sentence mentioned another Jamaican "Mamma", Mary Seacole; who had set up a private hotel/hospital hard near the battle ground of Inkerman, and housed in a large shack...despite being shunned by Florence Nightingale and the entire British Military/Political establishment. Her rate of success was vastly better than anywhere else in the Crimea, infection was virtually non-existent in her hospital, and her use of herbal remedies was very effective in healing the wounds; diarrhoea and cholera which at Scutari Hospital and elsewhere destroyed the whole army. In King George V Hospital in Romford, Fastovski had been berated by a ward sister for pointing out the presence of some staining on a radiator adjacent to his bed, and what appeared to be a small amount of congealed blood, which grudgingly received a rudimentary and ineffective "wipe over". The elderly Jamaican lady in the Romford Hospital seemed to Fastovski to embody all the energy, humour, humanity (and feigned bad temper when necessary) of these marvellous "Mammas", the finest people in the world. Let them, together with "Hattie Jaques" Matrons run the NHS and all will be well. Truly.

Whilst in the mixed general ward, Fastovski had refused to use the bed pan and would perambulate to the toilet past an elderly Chinaman who invariably would be sitting upright in the chair at the side of his bed wearing an oxygen mask. His white hair was chinese-stiff and full (somewhat like the elderly "Cato" of Inspector Clouseau fame;) and indeed very like the tonsure of Fastovski's best pal, "Cake" Wassermann the demon washboard virtuoso, and valued member of the Haroldean's second team which Fastovski had captained (see P118), and whose antecedents were in Sunderland rather than Shanghai. Having for a short time practiced the highly esoteric and deadly fighting variant of Tai Chi, Fastovski gave the elderly Chinaman a respectful bow, which was returned, and Fastovski would walk past in the soft fighting posture in his honour, which would receive another bow. This went on for a number of days; when having removed his mask it appeared that the old Chinaman, was not Chinese at all…in fact he was Welsh. Fastovski reasoned that the poor man was simply undergoing an identity crisis, and had probably come into the hospital simply to Dai.

Some years earlier when Fastovski and some colleagues were in the Rockie Mountains, he became very friendly with a wonderful character from Cardiff, Alan Jones; the greatest storyteller in the history of time. Probably most were untrue but amazingly entertaining. Jones prided himself on never smiling, and carried a wallet of photographs taken over many years to prove the point. His father, he pointed out was called "Dai" Jones…not that that was his name.

His dad simply could not remember people's names; even his own son, and so referred to everybody (family, friends and complete strangers) as "Dai"… "Hello Dai… "Mornin' Dai… "See you later, Dai…so he in return was named by his own family and friends (and strangers) in the village in the Rhondda as "Dai" Jones. A mutual friend related the story to Fastovski of Alans' chatting up of an attractive blonde new neighbour; who when questioned by Margaret (his wife) explained that he had told her that he was a war hero and that he been awarded the Victoria Cross during the Crimean War…(which had merely preceded their conversation by some 140 years). "Jonesy" would relate a most Rabelaisian and dissolute adventure which he and Fastovski had shared one night in downtown Cardiff which everybody still spoke about. To Fastovski's recollection, Jonesy had simply seen him off at Cardiff Station where they had shared a pot of tea. He loved the song "yellow bird" which he would sing in a strangulated falsetto despite being the possessor of a fine tenor in which he participated in a Welsh male voice choir. He explained that there was no other way to sing the song and had tried many variations before he settled finally on the correct interpretation. He sang it to Fastovski without moving a muscle in his face, through rigid lips and dead eyes a bit like a haddock, which he resembled somewhat.

There was a fair degree of sadism generally to be found amongst the staff and in particular one male nurse who administered the twice daily blood thinning injection into the abdomen with brute force and which caused massive subterraneous haemorrhaging…not dangerous but painful and which gave the appearance of being beaten black and blue. No doubt terrible things happened to other patients; especially the old and those with few (if any) visitors. The food whilst not bad was served in miniscule quantities which imposed a dependency on the patient which both weakened and placed them into a situation of subservience. Weight loss was drastic, and Fastovski in ten days had lost eight pounds, and some muscle. To cap it all on the night prior to his angiogram, the "Locum" consultant on the ward was a humorously stereotypical intensely mad elderly German who had presumably undergone basic training at Dachau and bellowed insultingly at the staff (which they no doubt deserved), and engaged a by now very weakened Fastovski in an argument about the "plight of the Palestinians" and the right of Israel to exist. Certainly not good for the blood pressure, and in literary (if not medical) terms, a case of Kafka out of Dr Mengele. Fastovski was assured by one of the more reasonable male nurses that he would be reported.

"Cake" Wassermann had grown up in the same street as Fastovski and were on "nodding terms" only, until they became close friends at the age of fourteen. It was the time when Fastovski had left the Synagogue choir and was sitting next to the ex-choir master "Ming the Merciless" when they were joined by "Cake" and they spoke about the hazards of shaving…which in those days was quite a procedure. After the service, they repaired together (with

Ming) to the reception held in the Synagogue Hall a most beautiful art deco construction as indeed was the entire Synagogue. Both Fastovski and Cake dined well on the copious amounts of pickled herring, sour cucumber. fried gefilte fish, poppy seed cake and "Jewish" biscuits. They also availed themselves of the dreadful Kosher sickly-sweet celebratory wine (a bit like a hideous parody of reject Port) until they were slightly tipsy, and at which point they switched to the more acceptable brandy which they "got down their necks" non-stop despite some quiet voiced concern by the good Ming, and a raised eyebrow (with a twinkle in his eye) from the inestimable Reverend "Willy" Wolfson…and more serious comment by one or two of the people who were paying for the party. By now, Cake and Fastovski had their arms around each other's shoulders and singing a rude rugby song whilst unsteadily descending the steps of the Synagogue with Cake holding a banana in his left hand.

Back past the "Lilac Domino" milk bar where Polly held court and the other Jewish shops and home to Brookdale Road where Billy Adams was standing (as he always did) on the pavement where it met Smithdown Road and where a passing young Naval officer had given a bloody nose to an antisemitic bully who was taunting a much younger and smaller Fastovski where great Uncle Shrolik Fastovski would walk in such military fashion with walking stick like a Regimental Sergeant Major at the age of ninety and where the huge Sidney Idanov who *had* been a sergeant major would walk down the road carefully avoiding the cracks in the paving stones and sometimes starting again and who bore a distinct physical resemblance to the comic creation Alf Ippititimus of

"Carry on Fame" replete with nervous tic and Tourette
syndrome utterances and where he no doubt remembered
that time as a child when he had tied up his mother to a
chair and lit a fire under it witnessed by Fastovski's
mother Tilly when a little girl with her own mother Lena
of the copper hair and piercing green eyes who loved
Jesus and for which event the young incendiary Idanov
gained a notoriety which remained to the day he died and
beyond and where "Oxy" Aranovitch the doppelganger of
the wall-eyed American film cowboy Jack Elam would
promenade in similar fashion to Sgt Idanov sometimes
nearly in step and where the jolly blonde Etty Stein would
waddle down the street with a huge chuckle and chest on
which she would laughingly invite the infant Fastovski to
sit and which he would readily oblige and where her
daughter the sexy and luscious Florry would walk with
her boyfriend and where her large personable sister Sonya
would walk with the even larger Nathan who had been a
sailor in the Israeli Navy and where Fastovski would
counsel one of the kids from the *frum* enclave of nearby
Borrowdale Road who wished to escape his orthodoxy
and had come to the right man for advice and where the
young Jewish Kids would eat Shabbos dinner of chicken
soup chopped liver boiled fowl and lokshen kugel whilst
listening firstly to "The Goon Show" and then "The Ted
Heath Band" not forgetting "Tommy Handley" and
"Workers Playtime" on the radio and in the afternoon
would stand in the violent "Boys Pen" at the corner of the
"Kop" at Anfield Stadium and do their best to avoid the
customary fights'(not always successfully) which would
break out and in the evening the boys would go dancing
to "Reeces" and try to "click" with the non-Jewish girls
(not always unsuccessfully.)

"Cake" had a marvellous spontaneous wit that complemented Fastovski's word play and surrealism perfectly. They relished "knock about" physical humour and were great fans of the "Three Stooges" and "Abbott and Costello"…as well as the Marx Bros; who appealed particularly to the more cerebral Fastovski. "Cake" played "Love is a many splendored thing" on the piano in an unintentionally chomping dull manner, and with an exaggerated "oom-pah, oom-pah" left hand which was very funny, and entertained Fastovski and wife on their return from Honeymoon in Ireland to an impromptu half hour improvised impersonation of Edith Piaf and Maurice Chevalier in a cod-French monologue/song accompanying himself on the piano whilst all the gang joined in.

Cakes father Sam Wassermann was the friendliest amiable man one could hope to meet. He and Fastovski would speak like mates despite the differences of their age and Sam would enjoy the surreal banter of the young man, and most forgiving of some of the scrapes that he got his son "Cake" into. He let things happen, trusted his friends and events, and quietly observed all of this from the bye line of life as it were. Cakes mother Dora hailed from Sunderland and possessed a strong "Wearside accent" and was a humorous quiet woman full of amiability like her husband and her son "Cake". During the war, Sam had served as a Prison Camp Guard in the Orkneys where he became on very good terms with the German prisoners. Sam spoke to them in Yiddish and would treat them with kindness and generosity. At the end of the war, one of the officers presented Sam with the iron cross of a dead soldier as an expression of gratitude which Sam accepted honourably and which he kept in his piano stool on the velvet "Tallit Bag" in which Jews would keep their prayer shawl and phylacteries, which to a traditional Jew was treated with veneration. Fastovski would laugh with the Wassermanns about this and fantasise with Sam as to his unrevealed and secret role as "Fieldmarshal Wassermann of the Wermacht". Sam would not see anything inconsistent in this seeming juxtaposition of opposites, which might horrify others who did not know him. It was discovered after the war that some three hundred thousand German "mischling" (mixed parent) Jews served in the German armed forces, and in very many cases as an avenue of escape from what was happening to the Jewish civilians in Germany. The blue-eyed blond Jews were very often sheltered in the SS; including many full Jews (including Helmudt Schmidt, who later became Chancellor of Germany,) Field Marschall Milch who served on the German General Staff was "Excused Jewishness" by written order of Der Fuehrer as was indeed the feared and fanatical Admiral Lutjens who served on the Battleship "Bismark" There were some two hundred senior officers from Field Marshal down to Colonel who were in this category. Thousands of German Jews served in the British Army, with a large number used in intelligence and interrogation; with many in the Commandos (some in Jewish units) which would serve in under- cover activity at Dieppe and elsewhere. One German Jewish Unit raided Tobruk deep in Rommel's rear, attired in Wermacht uniform, and the 51st Royal Marine (Middle Eastern) Commando comprised Polish and German Jews stationed in Palestine including the giant warrior, Zvi Sveht. German and other Jewish soldiers captured by the Nazis

169

on the western front were (in the main) treated in accordance with the Geneva convention and would not suffer harm. Some four hundred soldiers from the "Palestine Regiment" which was solely Jewish and soon to be renamed "The Jewish Brigade" (there being only a few Arab "Palestinian" volunteers); were captured in the fall of Greece were thus well treated. By comparison the Greeks handed their large Jewish population of Salonika (including many ex-soldiers of the Greek Army) over to the Nazis with zealous co-operation and transported them to Auschwitz.

They appeared to have forgotten that in the heroic resistance of the Greek army to Nazi invasion, a high percentage of their own Officer Corps were Jewish. The Germans behaved somewhat differently, as is well documented; on the eastern front, and captured Russian Jewish soldiers were slaughtered along with their non-Jewish comrades.

Sam Wassermann would have been unaware of most of this at the time. He had neither received nor accepted the iron cross in some modern politically correct gesture of "reconciliation" which is now prevalant in our collapsing society; nor in some ludicrous and hypocritical manifestation of Christian "forgiveness" and "inclusiveness" which is the lubricant of the multicultural mayhem drawing us all into its abyss. No, he accepted the iron cross because respect and friendship had grown between himself and the German Soldiers…and to Sam that is all that mattered.

The Turkish food orderly in the hospital in Romford; a loud and humorous lady; would wheel the trolley shouting, "Kosher...kosher!" possibly to reassure the Jewish patients who preferred this option. Fastovski however found the food too savoury and was on a strict salt and sugar free diet; so, he restricted himself to the standard hospital food free of fat, sugar, salt, carbohydrates, protein, vitamins, minerals and anything else likely to keep one alive. The "food consultant" to the hospital was the famed Lloyd Grossman who's strangulated vowels and bulimic appearance were no doubt caused by sampling his vile creations, and for which, Fastovski reasoned he should be indicted before a tribunal of geriatrics, heart sufferers and Welsh China-fantasists (not forgetting Episcopalians), and hung, drawn and koshered at Marble Arch (after being dragged behind a tumbril of soggy cabbage and collapsed carrot with which he would be force fed)...all the way from Romford.

The Turkish food orderly on one occasion could be heard perambulating with tea trolley from ward to ward relaying to much hilarity, an incident she had experienced that morning involving herself and an elderly Jamaican lady with very strong patois...thus:-

TFO   'What would you like to drink?'

EJL   'I'll have a brandy" (pr. **"bran-dee").'

TFO   'You can't have brandy.'

EJL   'Hokay, I'll have a Guin-*NESS*

TFO   'You can't have Guinness.'

EJL   'No bran-**dee**! No Guin-***NESS***…and you carl dis place a Hos-pi-***tal***?'

The angiogram revealed that Fastovski required a triple-heart bypass, but was prevailed upon to have angioplasty instead. A total of five platinum stents were inserted (about the maximum) and Fastovski nearly lost his life in the post-operative trauma. The operation, it was found later, had not fully succeeded; necessitating another operation some ten months later with a further three stents. He had required a quadruple bypass but was not availed this time of the option due to the very high-risk category in which Fastovski now resided. Fastovski later learned that in the second procedure he had in fact been suffering from pneumonia which had neither been diagnosed nor reported to the operating team at the excellent London Chest Hospital by the incompetent sadists of the King George V death house at Romford…and which accounted for the difficulties that the surgeon was experiencing, and the increasing heart stress and pain that Fastovski was suffering. He mouthed the "Shemah" while his head swam, and his mind returned to the frightening skull, followed by the large red horned bulls head/Devil/***Malchamovis/***Angel of Death he had witnessed when he had been rendered unconscious by a chloroform pad in a previous operation as a little boy. The surgeon however was good, and did brilliantly under the circumstances, and with some good fortune; Fastovski survived.

In a state of stupefaction and whilst in the recovery room, Fastovski rambled on about his heroes Long John Silver, Robert Newton and the Duke of Edinburgh who

172

always came back to him when rallying, and indeed very rarely (if ever) left his thoughts. The nurse asked him his name, and whether he recognised the two women at his bedside.

'Yes,' he replied, 'the lady on my right is my ex-wife, and the lady on my left is my soon-to-be-ex-girlfriend.'

'Do you have any vacancies?' replied the pretty young nurse.

Pam and Tilly at 'Polly's

Chapter Ten
The Red Shadow

Colin Hanson awoke from his troubled noisy slumber on the couch at 5am, swore, staggered over to his bed in the next room on which he threw himself in some palpitational frenzy only to be woken a few minutes later by his alarm clock; which he had (as always) somehow incorrectly set some time before.

He had nodded off at 9pm while trying not to listen to Nicholas Winchell droning on about the inactivities of the prize drone and arch-fool the pathetic Prince of Wails, but the combination of ginger muted aggression (from Winchell) and the fanatical passivity (of the future "King" of his Muslim Caliphate of England) was too much even for the rotund and ruborious Mr Hanson; who wisely accepted the only possible panacea…complete oblivion; or as near as dammit.

He had had a fairly normal day; had been misunderstood by virtually everybody he had come into contact with, and as a consequence had had a few "blazing" rows with the assorted morons, psychopaths and idiots who seemed to frustrate his every move. In this regard he seemed to share much of the fate with which his pal Fastovski was customarily assailed. He got on well with Fastovski not only for this reason of shared suffering but also because it was clear that Fastovski misunderstood him seemingly more than anybody else…reason enough. They also shared an office in deepest Basildon where Fastovski presided over the Government Contracts division of a major electronics company. On the first occasion that they had met, Fastovski had been ushered into the office already occupied by Colin who gave him a gruff "Hallo" and proceeded to bury himself angrily in the mound of files, papers, sandwiches (and apples which he would munch savagely), which can only be described, nay imagined in terms of the great Barricade at Saint Germain during the abortive Paris Commune of 1870 which had been so ruthlessly and bloodily put down by the dreadful Marquis de Gallifet… something with which everybody is familiar no doubt. Yes, his desk seemed to be a good thirty feet in height with a telephone or two (also seemingly well concealed, as would a Creusot-Schneider rifle have been at St Germain) ringing away whilst he angrily threw papers, apples and whatever all over the place to answer the call before it "rang off"…his score in this regard Fastovski calculated at 60/40 in favour of the phone.

Fastovski viewed this interplay of destructive energy and hopeless forlorn failure with a total lack of sympathy or understanding, but nevertheless with deep amusement…naturally. It occurred to him that some comment or other need be made both to confirm the absurdity of the situation and also to suitably enhance the discomfiture of the frenzied flabbergasted fumbling fellow. Fastovski quickly had ascertained that Colin spoke with a good old cockney argot, replete with occasional choice epithets which despite no doubt being acceptable in the environs of Bethnal Green from whence he had hailed; would not be quite "de rigueur" in the grillroom at "Claridges". At one moment when Colin seemed to suspend his frenetic activity, Fastovski responded with possibly the only riposte possible…and designed (he felt) to release some undercore of deeply hidden artistic sensitivity…or failing that to put him in another rage…either of which would have been quite acceptable.

'You're a right smoothie…AINTCHA!!! You are…the veritable Jack Buchanan of the World of Commerce…' said Fastovski. Colin looked up slowly, and his angry red face creased into a big smile. Fastovski was not sure that he had appreciated the comment; or simply happy that somebody was actually talking to him in something of a social context. It quickly became apparent however that Colin was a big fan of Jack Buchanan, and indeed was very knowledgeable about the whole world of theatre and variety; which his father had taken him frequently to imbibe in the heady atmosphere of the Hackney Empire, just around the corner where they lived above the leather shop in which Hanson *pere* plied his trade. Soon they were singing "Good night, Vienna" together in the clipped tones of the *oeuvre,* together with "I forgot my gloves" which the great matinee idol of the 1920's would render to his adoring audiences. Fastovski some months later was entertaining a valued client from the Home Office to lunch at the discreet and elegant "Bracewells Restaurant" at the Park Lane Hotel (where he was very often to be found)…and far superior to Browns' (certainly) or the Dorchester just about) or even the Savoy Grill at its best. Dick Johnson shared Fastovski's passion for jazz, and also for the light operetta of Frans Lehar, Sigmund Romberg, Ivor Novello and Robert Stoltz which Fastovski adored. They also shared a passion for Richard Tauber whom Dick had seen many years before at Covent Garden…and as the meal progressed and the wine was flowing and as the other diners disappeared the two broke into "We are in love with you, my heart and I" much to the amusement (and bemusement even) of the Italian waiters; who nevertheless refrained from joining in.

Colin shared the same patronymic as that of the famed John, who toured the United Kingdom in his inestimable production of Sigmund Romberg's well loved "Desert Song" which had captivated the West End during the inter-war period but had since the 1980s been considered somewhat passe…Great songs abounded such as "Only a Rose" which was later sung in BBC broadcasts by the great Anne Ziegler and Webster Booth…lovely singers who tragically were used in their later years as the butt of jokes from the generation that had replaced them. Much the same thing occurred in the world of Jazz where the great music of the "Savoy Orpheans" and Rudi Starita, and Fred Elizelde of the 1920s were now considered something of a joke. It was probably the same "mind-set" (to use a current colloquialism) that determined the destruction of much of Victorian London and Liverpool by the degenerate advocates of architectural "brutalism" of the 1960s – which without the heroic intervention of John Betjeman would have seen the destruction of the irreplaceable St Pancras Station. John Hanson, with John Betjeman, shared that vision of maintaining the beauty of great art, and of course he enjoyed dressing as a Sheikh complete with headdress, cape, jodhpurs, and long riding boots with whip…a sort of mixture of Abdul the Bulbul and Fotherington-Smythe of the lancers. In the Operetta John Hanson played the part of an aristocratic French Officer of the Foreign Legion, who would in reality be the "Red Shadow" and leader of the Rif Tribesmen with whom "Les Soldat de Gloire" would be in contention. Colin Hanson had therefore been branded "The Red Shadow" due to his surname and copper tincture.

Paul Eshelby, Fastovski's pal and considered amongst the top jazz trumpeters in the UK would tell a story (in his customary "Broad Yorkshire") about his first professional gig at the age of fourteen in an amateur dramatic society production of "The Desert Song" at Scarborough. The band were amateur, but stiffened with a few professional musicians, and the young highly talented Paul for a fee. At one point; as Paul relates, one of the "Legionnaires" on hearing a noise in the distance enunciates (in the Broadest possible Yorkshire accent)…'ark! I 'ear camels comin' over't yonder 'ill…which somehow broke the spell of magic which the other thespians had been otherwise struggling to weave.

Laura Beaumont the writer and illustrator, and one of the regulars at "Polly's" where she and Fastovski would chat about theatre; also related a story of her experiences concerning "Les Riff". Apparently, as a child she was helping backstage on one of John Hanson's touring productions at Bognar, where she lived, and where one of her duties (in a "walk on" capacity); was to bring on the great thespians "change of clothes" during a highly dramatic scene.

Unfortunately, instead of his "Red Shadow" attire, she brought on his sports jacket and flannels. Calamity ensued, and chaos, and expostulations, and tears, and laughter; young girl taken home by her mum (the wonderful Sally Barnes; a great if short lived Star of the 1950s variety) and put to bed with a ginger biscuit and cup of "Bourne-Vita" to console the wretched child.

As a young trainee teacher in Bradford, Fastovski had been inveigled into the staff Christmas concert/pantomime for the kids. He was obliged (a bit like John Hanson) to engage at one moment in a quick change (but off-stage) into a cat's uniform. During rehearsals, things went well. The backstage staff on this production were the sixth-form girls, and really not that much younger than Fastovski, and being "Saturnalia Season" getting quite flirty with the younger trainees on the staff. When it was time for his costume change, Fastovski dashed off; quickly adorned the "cat outfit" handed to him smilingly by one of the cheeky sixth formers…only to be greeted (after a short intake of breath by the audience) with howling laughter from the entire school. It took Fastovski a few seconds to realise that the Cat's tail, had been repositioned to appear at the front of the costume. It was a tour de force of the most superb example of the theatre of embarrassment…pure "Scaramouche".

Fastovski had always admired the Rif tribesmen, and indeed, the great heroic stories of the Foreign Legion of P.C Wren, such as "Beau Geste". Such admiration was never clear to him, when as a child they were portrayed in films as "the enemy" (best not be caught alive mon ami). However their brave and indeed heroic qualities were never written out as it were, and something indefinably romantic and noble applied to their image. It was only many years later when studying the savage Spanish Civil War and browsing through some pictorial magazines of the period that Fastovski learned something of an astounding nature. The Rif Tribesmen were in fact another name for the Berbers of North Africa; which Fastovski knew something about. He was aware that the Berbers of the Atlas Mountains in Algeria were descended from the Judean Tribes who, dispersed by the Romans after their third "Jewish War" found shelter amongst, and intermingled, with the indigenous population, and eventually were obliged to convert to Islam some six hundred years later…(some remained however as hidden "secret Jews"). He had, however, not been aware of their monumental struggle against Spain in Spanish Morocco, adjacent to French Morocco in 1921, and that the Spaniards had been thrashed by the small army of Abdel Karim the Riff leader who led a double life as a French trained engineer with somewhat of a reputation as "Boulevardier" and Café Sophisticate… Further research revealed that Abdel Karim had the same year pushed the French out of the Mountain area of Algeria, and parts adjacent in French Morocco and created his Riff Republic; which however was put down in great bloodshed two years later by a combined French/Spanish army of 250,000 men including air force units, tanks and artillery; against Berber light cavalry. No doubt Sigmund Romberg was aware of this fascinating story in the creation of his wonderful and enduring "Desert Song". On one occasion when Fastovski was chatting with Rashid, the manic chef at "Polly's Café" Rashid revealed that like Fastovski he hated the heat, and had lived in the Atlas Mountains and not in the torrid Algiers. He further confirmed, when the question was put to him that he was in fact a Berber, and spoke at some length at the different cultural make-up of his people and the wide differences with the Arabs amongst whom they lived but with whom they did not identify…and practiced a form of secular Islam in the main; very much like the Turks. He further revealed that there were still considerable numbers of Berber Jews within the population, and that the last ruler of the Independent Berbers in 600AD was a Jewish Warrior Queen who had given her life in battle against the invading Moslem Arabs.

This did not detract however from Fastovski's admiration for the whole romantic ethos of the French Foreign Legion which incidentally included a very high proportion of Jewish soldiers in their ranks drawn from the same type of international adventurers who joined anonymously in order to be granted French citizenship. This did not however deter the Vichy government of General Petain from disbanding their Jewish units and then dispatching them to the death camps of Eastern Europe. One such unit at Dakar in French Mauretania (loyal to General de Gaulle) had fought a large Afrika Korps force until they were out of ammunition, and were accorded an honourable surrender.

In the main, the Germans behaved honourably to the Jews in North Africa, despite their being enemies. In the main, the French behaved with characteristic cowardice, both in North Africa, Paris and "la France profonde" Nevertheless the French Jews found shelter and hospitality in the French Protestant villages of the mountainous central France despite the great danger that this had put them in. In Paris it was well documented that the resistance was almost entirely Jewish prior to the entry of de Gaulle and the Germans perversely acknowledged this with a massive "wanted" poster campaign with names and photographs of the "the Jewish terrorists".

Fastovski on one occasion had been asked to provide background music for a Jewish lady's eighty fifth birthday and held at the very "uber posh", "Inn on the park" in Mayfair, and was asked to perform the music of wartime France including "La Mer" and the songs of Jean Trenet. She revealed to him that not only had she too been sheltered in such a village during the war, but had been a member of the "Maquis" the French resistance…and had been "protected" by a senior SS Officer…which information she confided with a look that Fastovski found mesmerising… She had obviously been a very beautiful, brave and clever woman, and indeed still was…and knew life inside out.

**Granddaughter Jordanna, Fastovski, Daughter Rachel
and Grandson Adam**

Son Michael and Fastovski

**Daughter Rachel, Fastovski and Granddaughter
Jordanna**

Chapter Eleven
Confederate Liverpool

Fastovski was breakfasting with old cronie Edwin Marshal Klein, emeritus Lord Mayor of Liverpool. The previous evening Fastovski had performed his first Gershwin concert at the famous art deco Philharmonic Hall to great success, and across the road at the sumptuous Victorian Philharmonic Dining Rooms the two pals were now tucking into crisp black sourdough toast, thick bitter Frank Cooper's marmalade (the very best in the whole world) as Fastovski would surely claim; lashings of Welsh butter and steaming pots of smooth Colombian coffee…and languishing deep in the green leather "Chesterfields" in their customary style, which deviated somewhere between languid and manic somewhere between Beau Sabreur and Scaramouche and if truth be known somewhere between Rhett Butler and Lord Cardigan…

At some juncture after a little good natured banter and reliving the excitement of the previous evening, Fastovski confronted his pal with a photograph of the esteemed councillor which he had doctored slightly to present him in the uniform of a General of the Union forces of the American Civil War. This was paired with another photograph of 1865 taken by Brady himself of General

Ulysses Grant, C-in-C of the Union forces, and after Lincolns assassination, and the demise of President Johnson to assume the mantle of President himself. The resemblance was remarkable...indeed they could not be told apart. Marshall Klein did his best but with little success. In fact General Grant bore a closer resemblance to Marshal Klein, than Marshal Klein bore resemblance to General Grant. Truly.

Although the chums had together played much "good ol' boy" music of the South (including "Gruber Peas" and "Ellie Rhee"...) at the famous Cavern Club many years before in their "West Coast Skiffle Group" Fastovski at the time had failed to make this photographic connection. More remarkable still was the fact that at some point in his studying for his "A" levels at this time, Fastovski was ordered to take a three-week sabbatical where he was suffering severe nose bleeds due to overwork. It was not on the orders of a medico, but of his great teacher and mentor Leonard Curzon, English Master, intellectual, jazz trumpeter, and veteran of SOE who had been parachuted into Serbia to train Tito's partisans in silent killing. Both Tito and Curzon were heroes to young Fastovski. Tito included special units of Serbian Jewish Partisans in his armies, and Curzon himself was the finest example of Jewish Hero...good humoured, guarded, and with a pronounced faintly devilish demeanour...much like Fastovski himself in fact. On receiving his "marching orders" Fastovski decamped to Southport to stay with his grandmother Bobba Feldman after arming himself with a dozen or so tomes on the American Civil War which he had loaned from the American Embassy in Grosvenor Square, and which included many photographs of Grant. Fastovski spent his days in Southport studiously ignoring all things King Lear, Winter's Tale, Samson Agonistes, Oedipus **rex,** Aeropagitica, John Stuart Mill, John Milton, and John Meynard Keynes, and proceeded to bury his head in the battles of Bull Run, Chickamauga, Shiloh, Gettysburgh indeed all of them. He would customarily be found at the Floral Hall Gardens avec livre, listening to Military Band Concerts; the perfect accompaniment to the pursuit of war whilst reclining in a comfortable Deck Chair and enjoying afternoon tea with General Ulysses Grant, Robert E Lee, Stonewall Jackson, and Jubal Early… (Jubal Early! What a wonderful name…there is a name on a war memorial in a little village in Yorkshire which too is wonderfully poetic… "Jabez Mountain".)

However, the older Eddie is now like his doppelganger Grant a tad more grizzled…and the resemblance now stands out clearly in the pages of history… 'Well, I'll be damned,' said Eddie.

'Probably some connection on the other side of the sheet,' responded Fastovski, in a suitably drawling riposte whilst drawing languidly on an imaginary Javan cheroot. Eddie did concede that the American side of the Klug Klein Klan *(Klug…(yiddish)…streetwise)* had settled in the Deep South but there was to his recollection little contact with the North…however after a brief reflective pause they both agreed that on the evidence of the photograph there well may well have been some contact…somewhere… As was well known around Liverpool (and Everton also) the Kleins were a fecund lot; so such possibility was certainly a possibility.

187

Coincidentally, in his year of office as Lord Mayor, Eddie was scheduled to represent Liverpool together with a host of other dignitaries in a twinning ceremony with New York. Plans were well advanced for the party to be conducted to New York by the Battlecruiser HMS Liverpool. Eddie was to have stood alone on the prow of the warship as it proceeded up the Hudson dressed in full regalia with mayoral gown, huge hat and mayoral chain…a bit like Greta Garbo as "Queen Christina" in her great film of 1934. The New York Battery would have greeted the Liverpool Battlecruiser with a 21-gun salute, to which the great ship would have responded likewise, Mayor Giuiliani and entourage piped aboard by the Bosun, drinks in the wardroom, exchange of business cards, assignations arranged, drunks silently put to bed. Regrettably due to trouble in the Balkans the ship was diverted to duties in the Adriatic and so the event was cancelled. Fastovski's great dream to this day is to have the event rescheduled (with Battlecruiser and Eddie) combined with a Big Band Concert by Fastovski's Jazz Orchestra at Carnegie Hall. Best tho' keep an eye on all things pertaining to Serbian King Karageorgevic's descendants and the naughty Kosovans who have been infiltrating their territory much as the Palestinians have been coveting the territory of "their" Serbia…the heroic beleaguered State of Israel… The "Palestinians" have no name of their own for the land they claim as their own, yet hold 80% of this Jewish territory whilst the "ethnic cleansing" Zionists have a marginal 20%. Obviously for their pains in advocating carnage the "Stop the war Socialist Workers/Palestinian terrorist coalition" have earned their entitlement to the rest. After all, why behave like civilised human beings when murder and atrocity might get the lot? The Serbs have proved great friends to the Jews, and the Kosovans designs on the Serbs is exceeded only by that of the Palestinians for the Jewish State. The Palestinians have succeeded in destroying beautiful tolerant playful Lebanon all in the name of "Palestine" and tried the same tactic in proud and free Jordan which would not take their nonsense and where their terrorists were massacred in their thousands by the Jordanian Army...with hundreds escaping to Israel, begging for mercy and seeking sanctuary with their foes the "Genocidal Zionists". Kosovans and the Palestinians are the darlings of the limpwristed Western "Liberals" who bay with savage pleasure from the safe sidelines and lick their scrawny hate contorted faces at the thought of Serbia and Israel being "thrown to the dogs". Well, Sir... It jes aint gonna happen... No, Siree!

John Wilkes Booth son of Junius Brutus Booth and considered the greatest actor on the English Stage, turned over in his large comfortable bed in the sumptuous suite in the luxurious Compton Hotel in Church Street Liverpool, stretched; savouring the luxury of the fine lavender silk sheets against his skin, and proceeded for the next hour in bathing in the deep marble bath with running hot water then carefully and slowly stropping his ivory handled cutthroat razor on the thick black razor strop, He placed some juniper oil on his face and commenced his morning shaving ritual, slowly carefully wiping off the residue on a clean pressed linen face towel (being careful to trim his luxuriant moustache exactly so) then libating his thick black locks with lightly scented macassar oil. He regarded himself closely in the mirror, his 6'2" frame his broad shoulders and narrow waist, his large penetrating black eyes which invariably would lead to numerous conquests...and felt pleased with what he saw. He dressed carefully in Black frock coat with light grey stovepipe trousers, navy blue "weskit" and fulsome collared soft silk white shirt and plum coloured cravatte. On his head, he placed a large beige soft felt hat which distinguished him as somewhat "bohemian" in line with his thespian background, in contrast with the ubiquitous high top-hats then all the fashion...mostly blue/black with some of the "fancy" aristo gamblers and gangsters sporting light grey silk. He moved lightly and easily onto the grand staircase, nodding courteously to a fellow guest or two, and into the resplendent dining room overlooking the busy Liverpool horse drawn traffic; inspected the vast array of fine foods on display and helped himself to some chilled coddled cumquat followed by scrambled eggs, sweetbreads and devilled kidneys which he finished off with some sourdough toast and marmalade and coffee. Whilst enjoying his breakfast he lightly read the "Liverpool Mercury" with its up-to-date news from the American Civil War, and his casual regarding of his fellow diners revealed an agent of the Union with whom he was acquainted and another for the Confederacy sitting in fairly close proximity. After breakfast, the Landau called for him and conveyed him with his sturdy battered brown leather grip to the Liner at the massive Albert Dock, which was to convey him to New York where he was to kill Abraham Lincoln.

When the South voted to secede from the Union the scene was set for internecine bloodshed and horror on an almost unimaginable scale. The gun that signalled the war was one of a consignment supplied to the South by the Liverpool firm of Fosset & Co and used in the opening sally in the attack on Fort Sumpter, and Liverpool involvement henceforth in the support of the South both in men and materielle was simply enormous. Whilst the UK was officially neutral, support for the North was universal and powerful…except in one City…Liverpool; which flew the Confederate "Stars and Bars" from every Public Building and public house and many private domain, and hosted the Embassy of the Confederate States of America in a fine building in elegant Abercromby Square The imaginative and sentimental Liverpudlians from the most humble to the great Merchant Princes were enthralled with the romanticism of the courtly slow speaking agrarian Southerners. By the outbreak of the civil war, the Egyptian cotton industry was well developed and competitive in price and quality with that of the South…so there was never complete economic dependence on Southern cotton (as is commonly believed to this day) and cheap access was available to exceedingly fine cotton also from India. Identification with the old-fashioned South was simply one of admiration for this other-worldly people and the romanticism of their desire for independence which Liverpudlians would understand only too well. They too were "different". Liverpool became a hotbed of intrigue. Spies and agents from both sides frequented the Clubs and Salons, socialised politely and occasionally knifed or garrotted each other in the dark alleys and foul-smelling middens by the black waters of the grim River Mersey. In 1861, the United States and United Kingdom went to the very brink of war over the activities of the Port City of Liverpool, and Liverpool no doubt was at times in danger of intervention by the armed forces of the UK for their own seeming latent secessionism (top secret HM Govt. papers lying deep under Whitehall no doubt…never to be released.)

Judah P Benjamin, Senator of Louisiana was summoned to the Capitol in Richmond, Capital of the Confederacy. Ushered in by Stephens his Negro Major Domo, Judah was greeted warmly by Jefferson Davis, President of the Confederacy, and the somewhat sinister Nicholas Philip Trist, private secretary to Jefferson Davis and "eminence grise". Benjamin was offered the position of Secretary of State in the administration; a position of immense power and similar in many regards one hundred years later with the great Henry Kissinger another German Jew, of stocky build, warm avuncular disposition and immense intellect. Amongst Benjamin's awesome responsibilities were the organisation of the Confederate propaganda machine in London and very covert running of a spy network in Liverpool headed by the great James Bulloch, Southern Gentleman and by all accounts husband of the most beautiful woman in Liverpool. Jefferson noticed that Judah was a little bleary eyed, and not surprising for a man who had been up all the previous night enjoying "Hullabaloo" the annual Grand Ball given by the powerful Louisiana Jewish aristocracy; which mingled easily with the Great landowners and merchant princes of the South living in grand mansions and "riding to hounds" with their neighbours. Commencing in some decorum with fine wines and food, and followed by sedate and courtly dancing; at midnight the Ladies "withdrew" to allow the Gentlemen to become totally sozzled on "Jack Daniels", enjoy "hullabaloo" and engage in violent physical games including "English Rugby" with no holds barred, and played on the unforgiving marble floor of the grand ballroom, and some matched fisticuffs with wagers on the side. Judah was too heavy and now a little old for such activities so concentrated his energies in card games such as faro, picquet and "chemmy" whilst polishing off a constant convoy of Blatz Milwaukee Beer accompanied by caviar, cold roast duck; hot bratwurst (yessiree hot houndogs!) and soused herrings. By this time some of the young Bucks were engaging in horse races in the dark moonless night whilst a'hoopin' an' a'hollerin, and drunkenly galloping naked on the way back to rejoin their regiments whilst the stars shone in the firmament.

A great swirling mist had descended on the Mersey, and the portside gas lights were twinkling in the dark. Hansom Cabs were proceeding steadily along the Strand and Wapping Dock roads, and passing the numerous inns and brothels from whence emanated the sound of sailors from all the Ports in the world, with exotic and fearsome looking Malays rubbing shoulders with Norwegians, Danes, Dagoes, Chinks, Prussians, Russians and Black Yankees…freemen, who particularly seemed to like the Liverpool girls.

Indeed, many stayed and so started the Liverpool Black Community in the 1860s. No "slaves" in Liverpool. Numerous oil shops selling Lifebuoy soap by the pound, firelighters, sacks of coke and coal, paraffin, mops and buckets stood side by side with huge ships chandlers with their supplies of finest Scandinavian manufactured ships sails, ropes, spars, nails, paint, brushes, tar, sou'westers, seaboots, and the thousands of different commodities that catered for the vast shipping industry of Liverpool, second

City of the Empire. The fish and chip shops recently introduced into the UK by German Jews, were doing a roaring trade and discarded newspaper wrapping littered the streets accompanied by the detritus of cod or haddock and head shattering pickled onions, chipped potatoes and slippery jellies of green mushy peas.

Other vendors were selling bowls of scouse and pickled cabbage, hot meat and potato pies, cold jellified pork pies, scorching baked "Murphies", roasted chestnuts in massive braziers emitting a cheerful welcoming glow on the damp night, and giant "Bacon butties" about four inches thick with spicy brown sauce often accompanied by a great German boiled saveloy or cold Bavarian wurst. Big mugs of steaming powerful tea or Bovril were being dispensed rapidly to the mixture of toffs and their ladies "slumming it" with the Sailors, tradesmen, prostitutes, stevedores and dockers, who worked the Port. Others of a more insular disposition were sitting quietly in discreet corners, in the hostelries chatting in low voices…"fixers", adventurers, businessmen and international traders and criminals, and others who had a particular air about them which identified them as agents of the warring American parties. Softly spoken, confident and courteous they could be easily recognised for their easy athletic gait, gaunt faces and muscular bodies, and keen intelligence shone out of their fanatical eyes.

The handsome hirsute middle-aged German woke at about 3am and kissed his wife and drew her to him. 'Oh…my dear…my darling…that was so…WONDERFUL,' said Queen Victoria (somewhat later) to Prince Albert.

'Nein, meine kleine liebling,' he replied. 'It ist nicht mir who is zo vonderful…it is YOU meine kleine Englische Rrrrose.'

'Yetzt,' he continued, 'I must go now my dear…Ich mussen meinen boots put on!'

'So soon dearest?' she responded. 'Vell liebling,' he continued, 'it eppears zet ve…err…Englischer! Are about to machen krieg…err…go to Var…mit ze United Stades over zat Liverpool place…and I have been esked to supply some of my vise counzel and cool kopf…to keep thet Emericanische Johnny foreigner at bay…nicht war? Err…I mean Hey Vot! Jah! (laughs und schlappen der thigh mit pride und gemuchlichkeit).'

'Oh do be careful, dear Albert.' She breathed. 'Lord Palmerston…has ADVAISED me…that the current CLAIMATE in Liverpool is extremely HOSTAIL… especially for our Royal HICE…It MUST be your weak CHEST to which he refers… so do make sure dearest…that you pack a NAICE warm woollen VEST…'

Fastovski and Marshal Klein finished their breakfast and walked out into the gentle drizzle of the steel grey Liverpool sky where they hailed a cab; the latter to the town Hall; whilst Fastovski repaired to the Walker Art Gallery where he was to spend an hour regarding the old paintings which had been part of his life ever since he could remember. He felt a little unsettled however which he put down to his musing at breakfast over the death of Lincoln. He felt deep compassion for the poor man who had had a bullet placed in his head; inoperable, and from which he was to die in agony 24 hours later. In a strange and surreal manifestation of some perverted chivalry, Booth his assassin had chosen a one-shot duelling pistol; rather than say, a navy colt which would have shattered the President's head from any of six large bullets. Booth reasoned that a single-shot old fashioned steel ball would suffice to lodge deep in Lincoln's head leaving him virtually unmarked and bleeding but lightly. If he missed; or in the event of a misfire, he could consider that he had given his target a chance, and in that event he could consider himself a gentleman. This troubled Fastovski who felt the deep tragedy of the two men locked in this sensuous embrace of death…a good man having his life snuffed out…and an assassin's unquestioning acceptance of a singularly contumacious code of honour. He looked at the silver-grey wet sky, felt a sudden chill in his bones; shuddered; hailed another cab, and went back home to his apartment amongst the great brooding Victorian mansions of Sefton Park.

Fastovski posing at German Grand Piano 'Union'
(The Workers Bechstein) Bought from M. Bormann!
Romford, 1986

Ingram Content Group UK Ltd.
Milton Keynes UK
UKHW020100140423
420152UK00010B/348

9 781398 497559